North Antrim

Seven Towers to Nine Glens

Gregory Moore and Dr. Bob Curran

Cottage Publications

First published by Cottage Publications,
an imprint of Laurel Cottage Ltd.
Donaghadee, N. Ireland 2005.
Copyrights Reserved.
© Illustrations by Gregory Moore 2005.
© Text by Bob Curran 2005.
All rights reserved.
No part of this book may be reproduced or stored on any media
without the express written permission of the publishers.
Design & origination in Northern Ireland.
Printed & bound in China.
ISBN 1 900935 49 X

Bob Curran

Dr. Bob Curran was born in the Mourne Mountains of County Down but has lived in the North Antrim/North Derry areas for over thirty years.

Besides writing, lecturing and taking educational field trips, he has worked extensively with local community groups, teaching in both the historical and folklore fields. He has also acted as advisor on cultural policy and has served on a number of cross-border cultural bodies.

He has written widely on folklore subjects, in Ireland, Britain and the United States, and his books have been translated into a number of languages including French, German, Italian and Japanese. His publications include *A Field Guide to Irish Fairies, Creatures of Celtic Myth, A Haunted Land, Celtic Lore and Legend*, as well as *Coleraine and the Causeway Coast* published previously by Cottage Publications. He currently lives in Coleraine with his wife and young family.

Greg Moore

Greg Moore studied at Belfast Art College graduating with a BA in Fine Art Printmaking leading him to a career in design.

He only began to take an active interest in painting a few years later, after being inspired at a painting exhibition by close friend Patrick McLaughlin. Since then, his reputation has steadily increased, particularly in respect of his delightful pastel landscape paintings which are widely sought throughout Ireland.

A member of 'The Pastel Society of Ireland' and 'The Ulster Watercolour Society', Greg frequently holds workshops and classes for art clubs and societies throughout Northern Ireland.

Today he works in Ballymena as a Graphic Designer and has also illustrated two previous books *A Guide to Irish Wildflowers* and *Ballymena – An Illustrated History*.

Contents

Foreword

—: Tall Tales and Hard History :—

The coastline and hills of North Antrim have always held a special fascination for me. As a child, growing up in the Mourne Mountains of County Down, the northern coasts seemed both distant and exotic – another world in fact. Most of us spent our holidays in Newcastle which wasn't all that far away, but occasionally somebody would travel north, to holiday in Portrush or Portstewart, and would return having seen places like the Giant's Causeway and Dunluce Castle which, back then, somehow seemed very mystical and mythical. Some even travelled as far as the Glens of Antrim which was yet another world entirely. Once, I went on a bus excursion to Ballycastle which, to a small child, seemed to take all day and which was something of a major adventure. The memory is still of a strange new world, filled with history, fun and legend.

Of course that was all many years ago, and in those far away days I never dreamed that I'd be living and working along the northern coast and into the Glens. And yet the magic and the sense of adventure have somehow never diminished. The northern coast, the Glens and the lands around it seem just as magical and mystical to me today as they did when I was a child. And the more that I know about them, the more wonderful and wondrous they become. Written into the landscape are the history and the beliefs of the ancient peoples who lived here and their tales, deeds and insights resonate down the years, even today.

These lands are unique in Ireland because of their associations with Scotland. Some of them formed part of an ancient kingdom, which stretched across the Sea of

Moyle and into the Mull of Kintyre. This was known as the Kingdom of Dalriada, a name that has been preserved today both in a school in Ballymoney, a local medical service and a number of businesses all around the area. At one time parts of this Irish land may well have been ruled by kings based in Scotland whose armies moved back and forth between Scotland and the North of Ireland. Individual Scottish heroes too, travelled to the great warrior-schools in the North of Ireland, which were considered to be amongst the best in the Celtic world. They were to be followed by clerics who came from Ireland to bring the Word of God into the Highlands. Tales, songs and perceptions travelled between the two areas, celebrating the cultures of both, through the soldiers, monks and traders who came and went. A strong Scottish foundation was laid down in the Glens and along the coast, almost as far as the equally ancient kingdom around Larne. This was added to by Scots planters, fleeing persecution in their own country and seeking to acquire land in the North of Ireland. They intermingled with the native Irish and the result was a rich, complex but fascinating cultural tapestry which gives the area its character and which can rightly be described as its own unique identity.

It is not however, only the coastal regions, spectacular though they are, that have defined the area's character. The lands further inland – places like Armoy and as far south as Ballymena and Broughshane – as well as the East Antrim Plateau with its villages of Newtowncrommelin, Cargan and Martinstown – have also played their part. And in an area which is noted for its farming and fishing industries, it is perhaps surprising to find that iron and bauxite mining in Glenariff and Glenravel, has played a significant part in developing the character of some of the Glens people.

These are all lands of history. It was here that the Vikings came; that native Irish clans fought amongst themselves and with the incoming Scots over the land; that armies crossed and re-crossed and raised and demolished castles and fortresses. These were the lands of the MacQuillan, the Bissets, the Savages and the MacDonnells, who warred and fought all across them. These were also the monastic lands, of vanished churches and monasteries and some whose ruins were still said to harbour the ghosts of former days. Chieftains, monks, fishermen, miners, all have left their enduring mark on the landscape.

But it is also the myths and legends that characterise the area. The remote Glens, the lonely mountains and the shadowy river valleys with their pools and waterfalls are filled with tales and stories, some relating to bygone ages, others of the supernatural entities that lurk in the places that the sun fails to touch. This the realm of magic and mystery – where the mountain mist drifts along lonely roads and a single light burns away across the valley, through the darkness of a mountain night. It is the land of ghosts and fairies, of haunted castles and vanishing lakes. Here are the tracks of giants and the work of dwarves. In sun, storm or shadow, the coastline, the Plateau and the Glens are a strange yet beautiful world.

Sometimes the history and the mythology and folklore all blend together in a marvellous mix. Stories of great heroes or scholars such as Ossian or Finn McCool or Doctor Colville become infused with supernatural aspects and take on a quality that transcends mere historical fact. Places too, take on a similar quality. Tumbled stones on a remote hillside in a lonely Glen mark the gravesite of some fallen Celtic hero; the ivy-covered walls along a river, the place of a long-fallen monastery or fortress. This is a land where history and legend weave closely together. But in a world that is constantly changing, this is perhaps the last generation which will remember the old stories, the old ways and the ancient histories.

Which brings us to this book. This is a celebration of this area, which seeks to encapsulate its traditions, history and lore in both picture and text. It seeks to tell at least some of the history and stories of this marvellous area and to supplement them with visual impressions of its enduring beauty. It is only possible to give a glimpse of the rich and complex traditions of the area but any insight is a fascinating one and serves as an introduction to the region and as a keepsake of its undoubted charm.

So, come on a wondrous journey along the coast, through the Glens and across the Antrim Plateau and listen to the stories and histories that are to be found there. If I can share with you even a part of the abiding sense of awe and mystery of the place that I felt as a child, then we will have succeeded.

Summer skies, Kenbane Castle

The North Coast

—: Tales of Normans and Norsemen :—

The lands that lie between Portrush and Ballintoy are extremely ancient and full of history and legend. It was here that prehistoric men founded a tool works at the White Rocks, using a rich vein of porcelanite (semi-vitrified clay or shale) that ran all the way to Cushendall in the Glens of Antrim. The material was malleable enough to shape into cutters and spear-heads which were much sought after in the early world. From here too, men traded with a large axe factory on Rathlin Island, which lies between the North Antrim coast and Scotland.

Traces of these early peoples are to be found in other parts of the coast as well. At nearby Portballantrae for example, a large earthworks comprised of two circles – one exterior and one interior – have puzzled historians and archaeologists for years. This was a ritual site but what was its purpose? No-one seems to know. Another site in the tiny village was what was perhaps the oldest coastal watchtower on the North Antrim coast, perhaps dating back to medieval times. This was later replaced by a watch-house, partly constructed of the same stone as the medieval tower, but sadly this has now been pulled down by developers and no trace of it remains.

There are further traces of settlement dating back to Mesolithic times further along the coast at White Park Bay. In the hinterland above the Bay an ancient cairn known as The Druid's Alter was once to be found. This gave the entire area its name – Mount Druid, which stretched all the way to the village of Ballintoy. Again, no trace of this ancient site remains as all evidence of it were removed by an Anglican clergyman in the 20th century, who objected to having such a pagan relic on his land.

Perhaps one of the best known and most frequently painted sites along this coast, however, are the picturesque clifftop ruins of Dunluce Castle. Although often associated with the Scottish MacDonnells and the 16th century Earls of Antrim, the fallen fortress is much older than that. The name *Dun Laos* means 'strong fort' and it was originally the stronghold of the warlike O'Flynns, a Celtic family who controlled part of the North Derry and Antrim coastline. Around 1077, Cu Ultah O'Flynn was defeated by the Norman knight, John de Courcey, advancing along the coast from Carrickfergus, and his dun (or fortress) was destroyed. Two Norman knights – William and Richard de Burgo – were granted lands in North Antrim as far as Portrush and it was William who built the first castle on the site of the former O'Flynn stronghold. Of Welsh descent, he styled himself 'Gwillam' (William) and the Irish round about called his descendants the MacGwillam (sons of William) or MacQuillans who were to become the prominent family in the area. Styling themselves 'Constables of the Province of Ulster', they controlled an area that is thought to have stretched from the North Antrim coast to the valley of the Sixmilewater, near Antrim town. And Dunluce Castle was their power base.

The castle is supposed to be the home of a banshee-like creature that foretells death and doom for those who see or hear her. The tale, which was once widely told in the area, is now all but forgotten. According to tradition, one of the MacQuillan chieftains tried to make peace with his MacDonnell neighbours further along the coast, by offering his daughter in marriage. The girl, Maeve, was very strong-willed and was not at all enamoured of her prospective husband. Besides, she had a lover of her own. The Lord MacQuillan, however, was just as stubborn as she was and had her locked up in one of the towers of Dunluce until she changed her mind. This contest of wills dragged on for weeks and months with Maeve remaining in the tower and her father fuming outside. It seemed like a stalemate. At times she would sweep the room with a broom and at other times she would be knitting a garment, which she claimed, was her shroud, as they'd be carrying her dead from the tower. Fearful that she would carry out her threat never to give in, the Lord (who loved his daughter) arranged for her to elope with her lover when he himself, was apparently 'away from home'. In this way, he would save face in front of the MacDonnells. He arranged for an old nurse to set her free and for a boat to be in the bay below the Castle to take the two of them to Scotland. He, of course, would deny any involvement in her elopement. Whilst he secretly watched from another part of the Castle, the lovers escaped and departed for Scotland in their boat, but as they reached the open sea, a massive wave overturned the craft and both

Fading Light, Dunluce Castle

were drowned. Distraught with grief, Lord MacQuillan walked the beaches beneath the Castle's frowning walls and, looking up, he saw his daughter looking down from the window of the tower where she'd been held prisoner for so long. She was holding up the completed shroud. 'See Father!' she called 'It is finished!' With a howl of despair, the Lord MacQuillan turned away.

It is said that Maeve's ghost still haunts the Castle and can, from time to time, be heard sweeping out her room. She is also sometimes seen, looking out of one of the windows in the east tower and holding up her shroud. If anyone hears the sound or sees the figure, it signifies death within the year. One legend tells of how she appears in a photo of Dunluce, taken by a tourist and of how all who looked at it died shortly after. All photographers have been warned!

The ancient church which lies close to the Castle is dedicated to St. Cuthbert, abbot of Lindisfarne, although a legend states that the original dedication was to St. Murgan, a woman pulled from the sea by fishermen. The roofless building is not the original church and yet somewhere in the building there is said to be a stone inscribed with a seashell, taken from an earlier structure and in honour of St. Murgan's aquatic origins, but nobody has been able to find it. One stone, which is of interest, though, is a large deathstone, situated in the very centre of the burying ground. It is clearly inscribed with the date 1630 and marks

the grave of two children of the Burghers of Irvine in the West of Scotland, who acted as administrators in the region for the first Earl of Antrim. This has the curious heritage of being an English-style stone, laid by Scotsmen in Irish soil.

Off the Castle, in September 1588, one of the flagships of the ill-fated Spanish Armada, *La Girona*, foundered with a severe loss of life. A galleas, powered by sail and oar, she was the principal vessel of the Armada's Naples Squadron and was capable of comfortably carrying 500 men. At the time of her sinking however, she was carrying the crews of three ships (approximately 1,300 men) out of which only 5 survived. Damaged and taking on some water, she was heading for Scotland where it was thought that there might be some support for the Spanish cause amongst the Catholic Highland clans. Driven further out from the coast by cannon-fire from Dunluce and with her rudder destroyed (she had opened fire on the Castle, incorrectly assuming that it was English-held), *La Girona* struck a reef at the mouth of the River Bush and went down almost immediately. The few survivors were brought to Dunluce where Sorley Boy MacDonnell, the lord there, made arrangements to send them back to Spain. Bodies from the wreck were washed up along the coast for weeks afterwards and some of them were buried in St. Cuthbert's as unknown foreign soldiers and seamen.

On the north side of the Castle stands a tall hill around

which the main coastal road splits into two. This is known locally as Hangman's Hill and was once the site of a public gallows. This area of coast was once the site of a sizeable settlement and was the main administration centre since MacQuillan times for the lands, which stretched down through Antrim towards Lough Neagh. Traces of the foundations of old buildings can still be seen in some of the neighbouring fields. It was to Dunluce that many criminals were brought to receive justice and it was on Hangman's Hill that many of them met their end. When the coastal road was being built no workmen could or would cut through it, whether due to the thickness of the rock or to local superstition concerning the former gallows, and so the road was split around the hill. It is, today, a grim reminder of former times when Dunluce was a formidable power on the North Antrim coast.

Legends of giants abound throughout the area. Mythical creatures such as the Fee-ack and the Jarigans (an ogre with squeaky boots) were said to dwell in the caves along the coast, making queer noises, which resembled the sea booming against the rocks or the calls of hidden birds. There were also historical giants too, such as the massive but weak-minded Gilbert McLoughlin, who worked on the Earl of Antrim's estate in the 1700s and who was known as 'Lord Antrim's Fool'. Able, it was said, to run faster than a galloping horse, he carried messages for the Earl and accompanied the hunt. In all his life, it was told, he had never slept in a house but preferred to rest upon the hillsides in the open air. He met his end, falling off a cliff near the White Rocks.

The most famous giant in the area must be Finn McCool who allegedly built what is now one of Northern Ireland's premier tourist attractions, the Giant's Causeway. This unusual geographic feature comprises an area of hexagonally-shaped rocks seeming to stretch out into the ocean. According to legend, this causeway was constructed by the celebrated Finn McCool as a crossing to the island of Staffa, which was the home of his mortal enemy, the Scots giant Benandonnar. The Scottish ogre also started building a causeway (and there is a smaller version at Fingal's Cave on the island) but the two of them met in the centre and their fighting destroyed almost their entire handiwork. The remnants of their mighty construction (in reality created by extremely ancient volcanic activity) have drawn visitors to the area from around the late 1600s in order to stare at these gigantic blocks. Upon completing the mammoth task, Finn was said to have accepted the Christian faith and became a holy hermit, retreating to one of the sea caves along the coast. Because of his sinful past as a giant, says the legend, he vowed that he would never eat food that was given to him by human hands. However, due to his abject contrition, God sent a seal to him each day with a fish in its mouth so that the ailing giant could have some sustenance. One fish a day, nevertheless, was not enough to keep him alive – he was a giant after all – and after roughly a year in the cave, he passed away. Loyal Christians are said to have buried his massive body in a secret grave, somewhere on the headland of Runkerry.

Although the Causeway is well-known across the world and is certainly an awe-inspiring geological phenomenon, it is not completely unique. Apart from the shorter 'causeway' on the Island of Staffa there is yet another in Vietnam and some basalt pillars, thrown up in the same way, form the Devil's Tower in Wyoming U.S.A. Nonetheless, the pillars beyond Dunluce Castle are one of the wonders of Britain, if not Western Europe and their reputation continues to draw tourists from all over the world, each year.

Dunluce, of course, is not the only fortification on the coast – nor may it be the oldest – for the area is littered with the remnants of castles, earthworks and churches, some of considerably ancient date. An even older fortress may be Dunseverick Castle, the present ruins of which were once held by the O'Cahan family. Local tradition, however, states that there was a much older fortress on the site belonging to Sobairce, a High King of Ireland and reputedly the first man in the country to ride in a wheeled vehicle (a chariot). Dunseverick (which takes its name from this king – Sobairce's fort) was his summer palace and a great road was said to run all the way from Tara in County Meath (other versions state that it ran all the way from the

Rock of Cashel in County Tipperary), so that the king could visit this place. At the time of St. Patrick, the legend goes on, several extremely holy artefacts were deposited there – the Veil of the Virgin and the relics of Peter and Paul. These were given into the care of a local saint, Olcan of Armoy, who later passed them on into the custody of the O'Cahans. These artefacts have since disappeared although they are reputedly still hidden somewhere in the locality, waiting to be discovered.

A persistent legend about the fortress is that of Turlough O'Cahan and the Viking. Sometime during the 12th century Turlough O'Cahan was master of Dunseverick and overlord of the lands around. Answering a holy call from the Pope, he set off to fight in the Crusades against the Turks, leaving his sister in charge of his fort and lands. For years nothing was heard of him and it was assumed that he'd died in battle. When he'd been gone for many years, a Viking ship landed in the bay beneath Dunseverick Castle. It carried a Viking jarl (local ruler) named Haakon who was reputedly the grandson of Magnus Barefoot, King of Westfold in Norway, who'd been killed at Portrush around 1102. He was greatly taken with Turlough's sister and she with him and she agreed to marry him on the understanding that he became a Christian. This would effectively make Haakon master of the O'Cahan fort and the lands around it and he readily agreed to accept the Christian faith. Everything was set for a happy occasion

Morning mist, Giant's Causeway

– but there was one fly in the ointment. On the eve of the wedding Turlough O'Cahan came home. He had been held prisoner by the Turks for a number of years but had finally managed to escape and, with a band of followers, set sail for North Antrim. Landing at a place known locally as Port Cammon (the herring port, near present-day Bushmills), he intended to surprise his sister. Instead it was he who got the surprise on hearing that his lands would pass into the hands of the Viking, and he was determined to stop this happening. He secreted both himself and his followers in Dunseverick fort and, as the Viking knelt to receive the Christian baptism, Turlough O'Cahan sprang out bombarding him with Greek fire (a terrible burning substance similar to napalm, which he had obtained in the East). The fortress went up in flames and both Haakon and Turlough O'Cahan perished. In grief, the girl who had been at the centre of the affair hurled herself from the cliffs and she too was killed. The whole sorry episode would affect the O'Cahans of the area for years to come. The present ruins are not from Turlough O'Cahan's stronghold but rather are the remains of a 17th century coastal fortress, which had been built to guard against attack from Scotland but which was destroyed by Major-General Robert Monro and his Covenanting Army around 1642.

Castles and forts are not the only ancient structures in the area. Above the tiny inlet of Portbraddon stands the ruined church at Templastragh. It is said that this church is one of the oldest on this coast. There are many meanings given for the name – for example, Lesair's Church – but the spot is generally referred to as the Church of the Flame. The ruins on the headland date from the 1600s but it is said that there was a far older building on this site, which was reputedly constructed during the first days of Christianity. Tradition states that this was originally built a little way from the site of the present ruin on the location an old pagan graveyard. When it was partly built, the builders retired for the night and, on returning in the morning, found the stones that they had erected, pulled down and scattered all around the clifftop. They rebuilt them but the next morning they were overthrown again. Rebuilding it once more, they drew back a little way as soon as night fell to see what was happening. Once again the stones were tumbled over by an invisible force and a curious pale flame flickered in the very centre of the ruin. A supernatural voice then told those watching to build their church elsewhere. This they did and named their church Templastragh after the peculiar flame which had appeared. A well near the church was supposed to be especially holy and it is said that St. Patrick baptised 9 saints and 9 bishops there, including St. Olcan. Templastragh may have been one of the Seven Churches of St. Fechtany, which were scattered across the countryside between the Giant's Causeway and Glenarm Bay. The land on which the ruin now stands is said to be privately owned by the descendants of local families into whose care Patrick had given the original building.

Still waters, Portbraddon

The major town in the area is Bushmills, famous for its whiskey distillery, situated on the River Bush. This was originally a settlement known as St. Columb's Rill (an old legend says that St. Columcille blessed the water there, making it 'the sweetest in all Ireland') and in the 13th century was controlled by Sir Robert Savage, a tenant knight of the MacQuillans. It was Sir Robert who is first recorded as giving his troops a measure of 'aqua vitae' (whiskey) before going into battle, showing that there was some distilling going on in the area even then. Today the town lies on the edge of the MacNaghten estate.

The MacNaghtens were a Scottish family who had originally come from Morayshire but who had been granted lands around Lough Fyne near Irvine, by the Scottish king, Malcolm IV. However, by backing the Comyns against Robert the Bruce at the beginning of the 14th century, the latter deprived them of much of their estate when he became Robert I of Scotland. Their lands around Irvine were restored to them by Robert's son, David II but they never enjoyed the power that they had formerly held. In the late 17th/early 18th century (some Scottish historians date this around 1691), in an attempt to regain some of their influence, John MacNaghten, the 17th Laird, entered into a marriage with the Campbells of Ardkinglas. He had fallen in love with Campbell's youngest daughter and she with him. The Campbells raised no strong opposition and the wedding went ahead amid great celebration. From

several days beforehand there was heavy drinking amongst the men and the women, which continued right through the ceremony. When John MacNaghten eventually sobered up, a day after the wedding he found, to his horror, that he had married the wrong girl – he had wed Campbell's eldest daughter instead of the youngest. The younger girl was just as horrified as he was and together they fled to North Antrim where John worked for his kinsman by marriage, the Earl of Antrim. There were already MacNaghtens living in the North Antrim area at that time – Black John MacNaghten had come as Secretary to the first Earl in 1580 – but they held lands around Benvarden near Coleraine. The Earl welcomed them and gave them a small portion of land near Bushmills. However, because John MacNaghten had technically committed incest by running off with his sister-in-law, the Clan was stripped of its title and status. It was not until 1818 that Edmund A. MacNaghten of Bushmills applied to Lord Lyons, the Heraldic King at Arms to have the title restored. This was agreed and the Clan seat moved to Bushmills. Today, Bushmills is a busy town and boasts one of the major whiskey distilleries in Ireland.

The other main settlement in the area is the village of Ballintoy. The coast that lies between Dunseverick and Ballintoy is filled with odd rock formations and deep caves and lends itself to tales of monsters and terrible creatures. One of these was supposed to be a great serpent, known

Quiet harbour, Ballintoy

as the *Lig-na-Paiste* (*paiste* is simply the Irish word for 'serpent') which St. Patrick overlooked when he cast the snakes out of Ireland. An old Irish name for the creature was *Shony,* which was also the name of a Celtic sea-god, which was worshipped on Islay, not that far away. When the Normans arrived in the area, they referred to the creature as Shellicoat and said that it dwelt in the caves that were around Ballintoy. They also claimed that it wrecked some of their shipping along the North Antrim coast and the queer ocean currents around the area were attributed to its movements underwater. Tradition says that the monster could only be defeated by someone whose name was McCurdy, whose wife and mother had both been McCurdys in their maiden name – the name is still quite common in the area and the women of the clan are believed to have mysterious and magical powers. In the context of the battle there were certain procedures to be observed. The man had to be wrapped in the skin of a bull calf and he had to carry a club in which three nails had been driven which had never shod a horse. Even then, he could not kill the beast but only suspend it and it could return again after a hundred years had elapsed. The last person to reputedly defeat the monster was John McCurdy in 1905/1906, so anyone swimming around Ballintoy should be extremely careful!

Close to Ballintoy Harbour are a series of strangely shaped mounds and hollows. Although these are most probably the results of ancient volcanic activity, strange legends have grown up around the area. It was said, for example, that this was the site of a massive prehistoric city that was cursed by St. Patrick because of the wickedness of its inhabitants. Responding to the saint's call, God in His judgement turned the entire city to stone and the outlines of its former buildings and archways can still be seen today.

There is also some tradition that the village itself and some of the lands around it are actually part of Norway under an ancient agreement. It is said that during the 11th century, the area paid a 'tribute' of 200 sheep to Eystin Orre, Viking jarl (local ruler) of Orkney and through him paid subservience to Harald Hardrada, King of Norway and Denmark. The sheep were supposedly left on nearby Sheep Island for the Vikings to collect and in return, they left the tiny settlement alone. This in effect made Ballintoy part of Norway and it supposedly was never handed back. Although this is a rather beguiling notion, it's questionable as to whether it's true. But the name *Baile an Tuath* (Ballintoy – the town of the Tuath) suggests that there may have been some form of rule from outside the area. In Celtic Ireland, a tuath was a minor portion of land or a section of a kingdom that was held by a sub-chieftain for his overlord. The tuath referred to here might have been part of an ancient kingdom, possibly made up of minor holdings, which stretched across the Sea of Moyle and into Scotland. This kingdom was known as Dalriada and comprised areas along the North Antrim coastline as well as in Kintyre and in Argyll. Tradition records one of the kings of the Ballintoy region as having the name Maelderg, which simply means 'Red Chieftain'. This, it is thought, has, down the years, translated into the English name 'Reid', a name that is still quite common in the area. In fact, some have suggested that nearby Carrickarade or Carrick-a-rede Island takes its name from this family (Reid's Rock). However, the name is more likely to derive from the Irish meaning 'the rock of casting' or 'the rock of throwing', since fishermen have used the stack-like island as a place from which to cast or throw their nets since prehistoric times. Although still in use as a fishing spot, the place is now more famous as a tourist attraction because of the famous rope-bridge, which connects the island with the mainland.

Whether or not the area was once part of Norway, there are many instances of Viking settlements scattered through it. Old maps show a coastal region, between Portbradden and Ballintoy which bears the name Danescroft and it is possible that this was some sort of stronghold with a surrounding farming area occupied either by Vikings or half-Vikings – those who had married amongst the Irish. These people are believed to have traded with large Viking bases on the island of Lewis in the Western Isles and with Argyll, parts of which were held at certain periods by the Norsemen. So it is possible that the Vikings were

pretty well established here and this may give some sort of credence to the old notion that Ballintoy was somehow connected with Norway. Vikings certainly also raided along this coast, drawn perhaps by the monasteries and holy houses on nearby Raughery (Rathlin Island) that was also sometimes known as *Inis Menagh* (the Island of the Monks). Tales of raids and battles against Viking hordes still persist in the country between Dunseverick and Ballycastle.

Today Ballintoy has a peaceful, almost sleepy air but this has not always been the case. The exceptionally pretty white Anglican church on the way to the harbour was once the scene of a brutal and ferocious siege. The area was also the site of a relatively large castle built around 1580 by the Stewart family, possibly on the ruins of an earlier Norman stronghold. The family had come from Scotland as part of a general influx of Presbyterians, all along a stretch of North Antrim coast, and in the mid-1600s, Archibald Stewart was one of the land stewards in the region for the Earl of Antrim. In 1641, as the Irish Rebellion exploded all across the North, Catholic militiamen from the Glens of Antrim, surged all along the coast, attacking centres of Presbyterian and Anglican settlement there. The insurgents, led by James McColl MacDonnell (sometimes known as 'James of the Glens' and a relative of the Earl of Antrim) descended on the village whilst Archibald Stewart was away in Coleraine. They attacked the castle, which was bravely defended by William Fullerton, a member of another prominent family in the area. The Fullertons had come to Ireland from North Ayrshire, shortly after the Stewarts (around the early 1500s) and had taken land around the Ballintoy area. Despite a desperate defence, Fullerton and the villagers were forced to abandon the castle and take refuge in the church where they were besieged by the insurgents. A standoff developed during which James McColl vowed that he would starve those within the church into submission and surrender. Things looked grim for the defenders. However, a local Catholic priest, a Father McGlaime, a man noted for his humanitarianism, suggested that they might give water to the women and children who were trapped within the church. James McColl agreed and water was hauled up in barrels into the church tower. What none of the besiegers knew was that the barrels had false bottoms and that the priest and his followers had concealed oaten meal in them. This enabled the defenders to make themselves porridge within the church and so sustain themselves. After some time, the siege showed no sign of breaking and James McColl withdrew towards Ballycastle, allowing those within the church to re-emerge. When it was discovered what Father McGlaime had done, the priest was murdered by some of the militiamen who tried to return to take the village. By this time, however, an army was marching up the coast in order to lift another siege at Coleraine. This was the Covenanting Army of Scotland under the command of Major-General Robert Monro, who scattered all the insurgents that it encountered. Monro, however, proved no less kind to Ballintoy than James McColl had been, for he attacked and burned the village, believing it to be a stronghold of the Catholic MacDonnells. He destroyed the castle, before marching on up the coast and it took the village many years to recover from his passing. The white church, however, today stands as a tranquil and picturesque reminder of those violent and bloody times.

The descendants of William Fullerton continued as major landowners in the area. A number of them helped to develop Ballintoy and one, Downey Fullerton is believed to have allowed a shebeen or drinking house to operate on his property. This later became 'The Fullerton Arms' which is today one of the major hostelries in the village.

From above Ballintoy on the top of Knocksoghey, it is possible on a good day to clearly see the hills of Scotland whilst on a clear night, the lights of Legavullan Distillery on Islay can be glimpsed through the dusk. It was on the top of this mountain that many Celtic warriors lit beacons to attract the attention of their kinsmen in the Western Isles. It is also said that signal fires lit on the Mull of Kintyre could be seen from here and in this way messages were passed between North Antrim and Scotland. This only serves to demonstrate the close links that existed between the West of Scotland and this part of the world, at

Evening light, Ballintoy

the height of the vanished kingdom of Dalriada and in later centuries.

This closeness between the two countries continues even today, with people from both sides of the Sea of Moyle journeying back and forth between Ireland and Scotland. A few years ago a ferry existed to facilitate travel between Ballycastle and Campbelltown on the Mull of Kintyre but recently has lapsed into disuse. However, it seems that it will restart again very soon thus strengthening the ancient links that have existed since prehistoric times once more.

Whilst strange and bloody tales exist around the Dunluce-Ballintoy area even more mysterious stories are to be found further on along the Ballycastle coast….

Ballycastle and Armoy

—: Tales of Seers and Seamen :—

Just above Ballycastle on the Ballintoy road, the ground is sour and marshy and littered with huge rocks. It was here in the 1800s that the poor of Ballycastle and those who died in the Great Famine of 1845-52 lie buried. Hidden away amongst tumbled rocks, a little way back from the main road lies the Pauper's Graveyard to where the bodies from the Ballycastle Workhouse were taken at the height of the Famine. These were the destitute from the Glens, many of them suffering from Famine diseases – typhoid, cholera etc. – who were transported from the Workhouse on the other side of town in carts and barrows, through the centre of Ballycastle at dead of night so as not to annoy the townspeople. They were then left, often uncoffined and unshrouded, in these boggy uplands, well away from the more respectable populace.

Because many of these unfortunates were reputedly buried without the formal blessing of the Church, the place is reputedly very badly haunted by their unquiet spirits. There is also a persistent tradition in the area that Neil Burke, father of the notorious William Burke (one of the famous Edinburgh body snatchers, Burke and Hare) is buried here, although evidence for this is sketchy. Most sources agree that William Burke's place of birth was somewhere called 'Orrey, Co. Tyrone' which is usually taken to be Urney, near Strabane. However, Burke's father was an itinerant labourer and it is conceivable that he might have made his way to North Antrim at some point. There is a further story that Burke's elder brother Constantine might also be buried there, although evidence suggests that he worked on the Union Canal in Scotland, was married there and was latterly employed as a city cleaner in Edinburgh. Nevertheless, the legend is an intriguing one, which adds a sense of eerie mystery to the lonely headland.

Ballycastle is characterised by the tall and imposing cliffs, which border its bay. The Silver Cliffs tourist site tops one of these, looking down on the harbour below. Although this is partly now a caravan park, it was once the location of Dunaneeny Castle, an impressive stronghold and one of the first-known such fortifications in the area. It must have once been an imposing structure and it has played a significant part in the history and culture of the area. In 1612, Hugh McNeill of Dunaneeny was granted a licence to hold a fair there. This, some historians have argued, eventually led to the Lammas Fair, which is still held in Ballycastle and which is known world-wide. However, tradition suggests that there may have been older fairs and markets in the area, long before the 17th century and that some of them may have been held along the tops of the cliffs. Indeed, the name 'Dunaneeny' means 'the fort of the fair or games' and it might have been that games and feats of strength were held here since very early times.

The broad sweep of Ballycastle Bay with its harbour and strand provides a rather picturesque holiday setting. At one time, the Bay was probably much bigger than it is today, stretching back to the lands beyond where the Sheskburn Centre (Moyle District Council offices and Ballycastle sports complex) stands today. Originally known as Port Brittas, it extended as far as the sinister and forbidding shape of Dun-na-Mallaght, which today stands on ground behind the Centre. Even the translation of the site's name has a chilling ring to it, for taken from the ancient Irish it means 'fort of the curse'.

An old legend connects this place with St. Columcille. Apparently, the saint arrived in the area and found a local chieftain living with a woman who was not his wife. Columcille admonished them both but they replied rather rudely and told the holy man to be on his way. Greatly angered, Columcille cursed them both from the top of the fort, turning them into herons, consigning them both to the Margy River and to an isolated existence. Whilst herons are frequently seen along the River, it is said that no two birds are ever seen together. Perhaps the saint's curse has come true. The sinister mound was also believed to be the entrance to either Hell or Fairyland and, around the early 20th century, there were stories of a young girl who vanished there and has never been seen since. It is further said that, on certain nights of the year – for example Hallowe'en – Dun-na-Mallaght opens and the forces of the Ghostworld spill out into our own, though nobody is on record as having seen this actually happen. In actual fact, the site is probably an old Norman fortification, built on the site of an earlier Celtic stronghold or ritual place. A similar mound is to be found at Dundermot near

A walk on the beach, Ballycastle

Glarryford (midway between Ballymoney and Ballymena) and there may have been one bearing a similar name at Revallagh near Bushmills, a location that was extensively settled by the Normans.

It was also from Port Brittas on Ballycastle Bay, that three legendary Irish princes set sail for Scotland. These are known in folklore as The Three Collas – Colla the Noble, Colla the Stammerer and Colla the Pasty-Faced. They had seized the throne of Ulster from their uncle and had tilled his lands as tyrants for over four years. It is further said that they held swordlands (lands to which they were not entitled but which could be taken and defended by the sword) as far away as County Louth. A popular revolt drove them into exile and they departed from what is now Ballycastle Bay for the West of Scotland. According to the legend, these three princes went on to become the founders of Scottish Dalriada and it was from the Three Collas that the MacDonnells claimed desscendency and traced their entitlement to Northern Irish lands.

Scattered all around Ballycastle are small settlements which extend up through the surrounding Glens of Antrim. Some of these have grown into sizeable villages. One of the largest is Armoy at the head of Glenshesk. Although a village today, Armoy was once an extremely important site. During the 2nd and 3rd centuries it is thought to have been ruled from Scotland – from Argyll – by a series of Scottish kings. In 474 A.D. St. Olcan (reputedly the foster son of Fergus McErc, a king of Argyll) founded a major monastery there. The site of this holy house is now occupied by the Church of Ireland church at the Lag, just outside the modern village. The circumstances of Olcan's birth form the basis of a persistent legend in the area. Fergus, the Scottish king (who incidentally gave his name to Carrickfergus – Fergus's rock) was visiting his lands in Armoy (generally translated as 'the eastern plain'). As darkness descended, he was riding past a pagan cemetery (some legends say that this was on the very location of the Lag Church today) when from its depths, he heard the sound of a child crying. Dismounting and drawing his sword – for he feared that this might be a trick of ghosts or demons to lure him into the place – the king advanced cautiously. Just inside the entrance, he found a freshly turned grave and the infant's cry seemed to be coming from there. Pulling back the loose earth, Fergus found the dead body of a pregnant woman. Although she herself was dead, the child was crying in her womb. Raising his sword, he cut the body open and lifted out the baby. Holding it up in the moonlight, Fergus muttered, 'Poor wee thing!' which translates into Scots-Irish as 'Olcan!' This became the child's name. Fergus took him back to Scotland for a time, treating him as his own son. Later Olcan returned to Ireland where he was reputedly baptised at Templastragh church, near Dunseverick, by St. Patrick. Some legends attribute the finding of Olcan to St. Patrick himself but whoever found the saint, they laid the foundations for a great Christian centre in North Antrim. There is little doubt that Olcan later became Bishop of the Armoy monastery and presided over an ecclesiastical See, which stretched from the North Antrim coast to the shores of Lough Neagh. Olcan is reputedly buried at Cranfield near Randalstown where there are the ruins of a medieval church dedicated to him. The monastery at Armoy flourished and is known to have had connections with other monastic institutions in Northumbria and Clonmacnoise.

One of the features which shows the importance of Armoy as a religious institution was the addition of a round tower, probably during the 11th or 12th centuries, the remnants of which can still be seen. This is the only surviving round tower in North Antrim. The See of Armoy, however, does not appear to have continued much beyond the 12th century. In fact Olcan is the only bishop that is known about. By 1117, another bishop was writing from Armoy – his name was Flann O'Scullagh (O'Sculu) and he was the Bishop of Down and Connor. The extensive See of Armoy seems to have disappeared in the ecclesiastical reorganisations of 12th century Ireland. There is no evidence as to when the monastery was dissolved but it is possible that the land around the Lag may be riddled with old monastic ruins. The 'layered' geology of the nearby fields may owe much to the retreating glaciers but it might also have something to do with an extensive holy house.

The present church was built in 1740 on the site of an earlier structure, which ran in a somewhat similar direction. Certain bones which have been excavated in recent times from a very old graveyard around the site, appear to show some traces of leprosy and it is possible that the disease may have been virulent in the countryside around the monastery.

Armoy was initially known as Welltown due to the presence of a nearby holy well, which was used by many of the local Catholic populace. During the Plantation period in the 1600s, there were suspicions amongst English settlers that Armoy's proximity to the Catholic Glens might make it a springboard for rebellion, and so in the mid-17th century, a fortress known as Castlebane (the white castle) was built near the site of the present Lag church. The village grew up to the west of this fort, the site of which had long since disappeared.

Buried in the churchyard at Lag are a number of prominent figures from the surrounding locality, but perhaps none so famous as a connection of the person who is laid to rest under a somewhat insignificant stone to the left of the gate. This is the grave of Rafe Wilde who was Vicar of Armoy from 1816-17. Whilst few might have heard of Rafe, almost everyone will have heard of his notable (and somewhat notorious) relative, the writer Oscar Wilde. In fact Oscar stayed at the old Rectory in Armoy at one stage and it was thought that this might have been commemorated by a plaque. However, given his subsequent notoriety, local people objected and this fact is not mentioned in the locality.

Back in Glenshesk and still in sight of the church, lies a pagan enclosure with a peculiar stone, inscribed with a design, which resembles a rearing serpent. Cast in amongst the bushes is a crude Christian cross, rather similar to one standing in a roadside hedge at Cuilfeghtran, along the road to Ballyvoy. This must have been a pre-Christian site of some significance but its purpose, along with any information concerning it, has been lost to history. Nevertheless, it remains a sinister and mysterious place of which nobody knows the true purpose.

Another such place lies in neighbouring Glentaise. This is a spot which is known locally as the Hanging Wood and is probably another old Norman fortification, now very much overgrown with trees and bushes. Tradition states that the place receives its name from the fact that certain local malefactors were hanged there, well beyond the precincts of any settlement. It is also said (although not proven) that the wood used to be the abode of a famous witch or seeress who was murdered around the time of the Lammas Fair well over a century and a half ago and who, from beyond the grave, took a dreadful revenge upon her murderers. Although this is just an old tale, some locals choose to avoid the spot and there is an old story that no human foot has trod in some parts of these ancient woodlands since the time of the Normans.

A little way off the Armoy-Ballycastle road at Kilcrue stands what might well be an ancient cursing circle. A number of stones have been circularly placed around one upright stone, which had been incised with a Latinised cross and is known locally as The Priest's Stone. Some legends say that this circle can be used at certain times of the day for casting curses against one's enemies and mention rituals for doing so. At one time, so the story goes, the original stones of the circle were scattered to make way for a neighbouring quarry and the Priest's Stone was used as part of a drinking trough for cattle. All the animals that drank from the trough died. Fearful of some supernatural repercussion, some local people tried to reconstruct the circle but most of the stones were now lost. In desperation new stones were cut from the quarry and were placed around the Priest's Stone. Although fascinating, this is probably no more than an old tale. The actual site is thought to be the location of a vanished church – probably connected to the monastery at Armoy – with the stone marking the entrance to an ancient graveyard. A similar stone is to be found at Drumnakeel – the ridge of the church – between Ballycastle and Cushendun. However, the ancient stone continues to exert considerable power and unease throughout the surrounding countryside.

Spring, Armoy Church and Round Tower

Another, smaller village lies a few miles outside the town on the road to Tor Head. This is Ballyvoy and the common meaning given to this name is 'the yellow town' although how it came by this name is now unknown. It may have been a portion of land given by the MacDonnells to Hugh Boy O'Neill (Yellow Hugh) for his support in one of their uprisings or the name may refer to something else. The name of the area is Carry which simply means a causeway or bridge and which was probably a connection point between the 'civilised' lands around present-day Ballycastle and the wilder and untamed lands, which lay beyond the Margy River. The original settlement of Ballyvoy may well have grown up around this crossing, which was probably used by people making their way from further back in the Glens making their way down to Ballycastle.

As a town, Ballycastle is comparatively modern, although it takes its name from an old castle, which was once erected in the very centre of the town, just off the Diamond, where the Church of Ireland now stands. This stronghold was built around 1625 by the youngest son of Sorley Boy MacDonnell, Lord of Dunluce. During the 1642 Irish Rebellion, this castle was briefly occupied by a garrison of the Marquis of Argyll's regiment who had driven out the Irish rebel Glensmen who had previously captured it. Following their departure, the castle became the centre of various disputes between the Countess of Antrim and the Stewarts of Ballintoy, although it is doubtful if, even

after these disagreements were finally settled in her favour, the Countess actually lived there. The fortress remained unoccupied and derelict until in the late 1700s it had become positively dangerous. Around 1852, Charles Kirkpatrick of Whitehall, an agent for the Boyd estate which then owned the land, applied to have it pulled down and permission was granted. What is now the Diamond (which would have been in front of the castle) was a barley field through which a small river ran, crossed by a small bridge, known as the Blind Bridge, probably because it led nowhere.

After the Rebellion, the entire area of the present town was almost completely deserted and controlled by soldiers stationed by General Monro at Dunaneeny.

Ballycastle, as it is known today, was initially laid out by Colonel Hugh Boyd who acquired the lands in 1734 on permanent lease from the 5th Earl of Antrim. The Boyd house stands on the corner of what is now the Quay Road and Mary Street and from the windows of this now derelict building, the family could look out on what constituted a minor industrial estate. Today, the tennis courts stand on the site of Glass Island, which was a major glassworks in the region. There was also a soapworks, salt refinery, ropeworks and an outer dock from which coal could be exported from nearby coalmines to Dublin. Colonel Boyd died in 1765, aged 75 years and left behind him a steadily

Summer pasture, Armoy Farmhouse

growing town that would become an important centre on the North Antrim coast. The town itself is a curious hybrid – not really a market town, not really a seaside resort and yet containing elements of both. For a remote country town it has elements of great sophistication such as the beautiful tree-lined Quay Road which Colonel Boyd had built to access his industrial area down on the sea front. In Ann Street – named after Ann McAllister, the Colonel's wife – is a small shop, formerly owned by John Henry McAuley, who wrote the famous song *The Oul' Lammas Fair* which has been recorded worldwide.

There is no Parish of Ballycastle, the churches there lie in the Parish of Ramoan, which takes its name from an area on the outskirts of the town. This contains what is perhaps one of the oldest burying-grounds in the region and takes its name from an ancient earthworks which stood there – Moen's Rath - which may well have been one of the oldest settlements in the Ballycastle area. It was here that the forces of James MacDonnell of Red Bay and his younger brother Sorley Boy gathered in order to do battle with Shane O'Neill, Earl of Tyrone, who had been set against them. The battle itself occurred just a little way from the site of the churchyard and on the edge of what is now a housing complex and was an overwhelming victory for O'Neill's army. It was this battle, on 2nd May 1565, that effectively broke MacDonnell power in North Antrim. The cemetery is also the resting place for members of the Boyd

family, descended from Colonel Boyd and great men and women in their own right. It is a tranquil and restful place, belying the violence that once surged around it.

Much of Ballycastle's trade lay not with its Irish hinterland but with Scotland and many of its major fairs and markets were attended by people from the Western Isles and from Kintyre. There are still many people, living in the town today, who can remember Scottish fishermen selling their catch along the Ballycastle quay. Recently, a ferry ran between the town and Campbelltown in the Mull of Kintyre, but it ran into financial and operational difficulties and had to be taken off. Nevertheless, there is now some talk about reviving it once more and it may soon be running again. Ballycastle, however, was for many years a port for Scottish sailors and the harbour was filled with Scottish vessels, both taking on and unloading their cargoes. Sadly, those days too are long past although the harbour is still a haven for small recreational fishing boats and a port for the ferry to Rathlin Island.

There was once an old saying in the region which remarked that 'civilisation stopped at the Margy River' which flowed just beyond Ballycastle. This may be suggestive of the argument that the Glens were once divided into two sections – the Upper Glens which comprised Glentaise, Glenshesk and perhaps part of Glendun and which were ruled by the MacQuillans and their tenant knight, and the Lower Glens which were the abode of wild Irish who were *'strange and unbiddable'*.

 In order to bring some sort of civilising religious orthodoxy, a churchman and landowner named Rory MacQuillan built Bonnamargy Friary around 1490 and invited monks from the Order of St. Francis to reside there. He had been appointed to oversee these lands following the departure of his predecessor Magonious O'Choinn who had encouraged the people of the Glens into idolatry and dark practices. Rory also took over stewardship of the Seven Churches of St. Fechtany that were said to be especially holy but which had fallen into idolatrous ways. The remains of the Friary, which now stand on the edge of Ballycastle Golf Club, denote a fairly substantial monastic house with a gatehouse and upper dormitories. Bonnamargy was also supposed to be a major burying ground of the MacQuillans though only one is buried there – Julia MacQuillan, the celebrated Black Nun. Details about her are scant but she is known to have been an austere and religious hermit. She is thought to have come to live in the gatehouse at Bonnamargy from the ruined castle in what is now the centre of the town some time about the late 1600s or early 1700s. By this time, the monastery was deserted, the monks having long since departed. (Bonnamargy is said to have been dissolved around the mid-1500s under the General Dissolution of the Monasteries, although there are records of letters being written from it as late as 1640). Julia's grave

was on the threshold of the doorway of the main chapel, so that those attending Mass would have to step across her resting place – the ultimate sign of humility even in death. Although she was simply known as the Black Nun, no-one knows whether this was because of the grime on her skin or whether it was because she wore a black habit (there is no record of which Order she belonged to if indeed she did belong to any Order). She was, however, known to be a religious eccentric and something of a local seer or prophetess and is credited with a number of predictions which are said to have come true. For instance, she foretold that two standing stones, five miles apart during her lifetime, would one day come together and this did in fact happen as they were used in the building of the original harbour at Ballycastle. She also predicted that a redheaded priest would come from far away to say Mass in the church at Murloch and would die the following day. This did not happen until the 20th century when the red-haired Father James McCann was drowned whilst swimming off Pan's Rocks near Ballycastle after saying Mass at Murloch, the day before. She made further predictions that men would one day ride in carriages not drawn by horses and that the air would be filled with metal birds – she probably foresaw motorcars and aeroplanes. One prophecy that still hasn't come true is that Knocklayde; the mountain (which is actually a dormant volcano) that rises above Ballycastle will erupt and will devastate the area around it for about a distance of seven miles. So if you're thinking of climbing the mountain, it might be as well to think again!

Although she has long been dead, the Black Nun's unquiet ghost is still said to haunt Bonnamargy Friary and many local people claim to have seen her. The ruins are certainly very eerie after nightfall and it used to be a great 'dare' for the young boys of Ballycastle to spend at least part of a night there.

Another legend concerning the Friary does not concern the Black Nun at all. It is said that before they left Bonnamargy, the Franciscan friars hid a great quantity of gold and religious ornaments in its grounds and that this treasure has never been discovered. For all would-be treasure-hunters, here's a tip from an old source. Take a candle to the main window of the chapel and place it midway along. Light it. The furthest point where its shadow falls is where the treasure is buried. Unfortunately the same source doesn't disclose how tall the candle has to be!

Just beyond the Friary and a little way from the Margy River lies the townland of Cuilfeightran or the 'Corner of the Strangers'. Just who these 'Strangers' were is a matter of speculation – they may have been Scots, they may have been Norse or they may have been someone else. The region, however, lies on the edge of the Lower Glens and is marked by the site of an old church which stood about half-way up the hill leading out of Ballycastle towards Ballyvoy. No trace of this now remains but this may have been one of the churches of St. Fechtany and was undoubtedly an early Christian site.

At one time the lands above Ballycastle leading towards the Glens would have been covered in thick and dark forests, although little trace of these remains today. One remnant, which can still be seen, however, is Ballypatrick Forest on the very top of the mountain, although much of this area has been taken over by the Forestry Division. Somewhere here are said to lie the ruins of a large stone house, which was once occupied by three gigantic cannibal sisters. These terrors were believed to devour travellers who passed by their door on the way across the mountain. The bodies of these unfortunates were then boiled in massive iron pots and their bones were buried deep in the Forest itself. The three were supposedly killed by several Highland chieftains who were returning from a battle against the Irish, somewhere near Tor Head. Their house was then pulled down and, according to legend, the tumbled stones still lie, covered with moss, in the dark under the trees.

The high mountain country also contains one of Northern Ireland's most curious geological phenomena – Loughareema, the Vanishing Lake. Because of the lie of the land and because the area all around is largely made up of porous limestone, the lake appears on some days

Brooding skies, Bonnamargy Friary, Ballycastle

to be full almost to overflowing and on others to have disappeared completely, leaving only damp and muddy ground in its wake. Water runs down from the surrounding slopes to form the lake (which is very deep in places) whilst the limestone surface allows it to drain away into the ground. Of course, such a curious phenomenon has attracted many folktales and legends. The most common one concerns a local priest and a bullying landlord. The landlord, it appears was charging his tenants unfair rents and was ordering them to do work for which he wasn't paying them. The people approached a local priest and asked him to speak to the landowner on their behalf. As the landlord rode along the road between two small hills, the clergyman stopped him and made his plea. The other contemptuously dismissed his entreaties and, raising his riding crop, knocked the priest's hat off onto a small hillock, as a mark of disrespect. Outraged, the cleric publicly cursed him, telling him that he would die by water where no water should be. The landlord only scoffed at this and rode on. Some weeks later, he was riding through the same place when his horse suddenly lost its footing and threw him. As he tumbled to the ground, stunned, water suddenly bubbled up around him, drowning him as he lay there. The priest's curse had come true. And every so often, the water returns, only to vanish again in a day or two. There is only one part of the lough that always remains inexplicably dry – this is the spot where the priest's hat fell to earth.

Certainly several people are recorded as drowning in Loughareema. The surrounding land, through which the road runs, is very steep and there are accounts – mainly traditional – of carriages losing their grip on the road and plunging straight into the Lough, their occupants dying in the freezing waters. One of these is said to be the famous Cushendall coach which was carrying the post between the Glens and Ballycastle. The ghost of this vehicle is still said to travel the roads on dark nights, its occupants dressed in 'bonnet, tippet and shawl', and to hear the sound of the post horn means death within the year. In one instance, almost within living memory, Baron Cushendun (who was an extremely strong swimmer) dived into the waters of the Lough to rescue some relatives who had fallen in. He was not able to bring them out alive though. The edges of the Vanishing Lake are reputedly haunted by the spirits of those who have drowned there and on certain nights of the year, queer lights are sometimes seen moving on the furthest bank, well away from the road. Loughareema is certainly not a place to be in the dead of a winter's night.

Near the village, at the foot of Tor Head, stand the ruins of Carra Castle, which was once a stronghold of the MacDonnells. It was to this fortress, in 1567, that Shane O'Neill fled, following his spectacular defeat by the O'Donnells of Donegal. The North Antrim MacDonnells were, to some extent, his own kinsmen as Sorley Boy MacDonnell was married to his sister and perhaps Shane

On top of the world, Fair Head

felt he could find shelter there. The MacDonnells initially welcomed him under the Highland laws of hospitality, which they adhered to, and even threw a banquet for him. As the night wore on however, and much drink flowed, an argument developed between certain members of the clan and Shane's secretary, Gerot Flemyng. Meaning to quell the disagreement, Shane himself stepped into the middle of the throng and was instantly cut to pieces by MacDonnell knives. His body was dumped on the hillside above the Castle, forever looking into Islay and Kintyre, the seat of MacDonnell power. For many years afterwards, the Earls of Tyrone continuously asked the Earls of Antrim for the return of the body so that it could have an O'Neill burial near Dungannon, and each time they were refused. In the end, a rather dramatic Celtic cross was raised over the grave, which was then used as a burial site by some of the O'Neills and their relatives. The grave can still be seen, standing in a field beside the Scenic Route, which winds its way over Tor Head.

In this area too stands Altagore Cashel. This ancient site predates the Earl of Tyrone and the MacDonnells and is a prehistoric stone fortification, which in many ways resembles the brochs (early forts) of Western Scotland. There is evidence that it was once accessed by an internal stair system. Such structures probably date from 500 B.C. – 1000 A.D and perhaps protected the settlement of a small family that may have arrived from Scotland. In fact, the land round about is dotted with the ruined cottages and abandoned farmsteads of Scottish settlers who have moved further inland, away from the exposed and windy coastline. Altagore is said to be particularly fairy-haunted with local tales of lights and sounds of fairy revelry around the old cashel and of strange and inhuman shapes, glimpsed in the twilight along the Tor Head road. Higher up on the headland, the dwellings become more scattered as the land becomes poorer, although there are still small clusters of houses, possibly originally the *clachans* (dwelling-places) of shepherds and herders which have become permanent settlements.

The land across the mountain and down to the sea is bleak and windswept, full of ancient forts and hidden bays. It is a land well-suited to tales of fairies and ghosts. It is a place of ancient and bloody history, with tales of conflicts and battles between the MacDonnells and their enemies. Such tales continue across the land, which runs down towards Cushendall and the imposing sweep of Red Bay.

On the road, Murlough Bay

The Heart of the Glens

—: tales of Scots and Planters :—

The pretty village of Cushendall, known by many as 'the capital of the Glens', nestles at the foot of the Dall River in Glenballyeamon. Although a County Antrim settlement, Cushendall lies only fifteen miles from the Scottish coastline, so it is not surprising to find a strong Scottish influence running through the surrounding area. Nevertheless the countryside around is filled with Irish history.

Between Cushendall and the headlands to the north, tucked away in a sheltered bay, lies the picturesque village of Cushendun. The name means 'mouth of the brown river' and marks the point where the River Dun flows into the sea. Several houses in the village are built in the Cornish style, designed in 1912 by the architect Clough William-

Ellis whose wife came from Cornwall. Other buildings were added later, designed by Frederick McManus.

In 1927, Ronald John McNeill was created First Baron Cushendun, taking his name from the beautiful little village.

Along the road which runs down from Cushendun, there are signs for Orra Beg Mountain and Ossian's Grave. This latter site connects the area with Irish myth, for Ossian was the most famous of all Irish poets, a Knight of the Red Branch and the son of Fionn MacCumhaill (Finn McCool) who was allegedly not only a giant but a heroic figure in ancient Ireland. Ossian's poetry was reputedly the most beautiful in the world, so much so that it charmed the heart of the fairy queen living in the Otherworld. She lured Ossian away to her own realm where she offered to make him her husband if he would live with her forever. Reluctantly Ossian agreed but after the first week had passed, he found himself pining for his homeland in Ireland. He begged his fairy mistress to let him return – if only for a day – and grudgingly, she did so. She gave him her fairy horse but warned him that he must never dismount from it, nor allow any part of his body to touch the earth and that he must return before nightfall. So Ossian returned to the mortal world on the slopes of Orra Mountain. Although only a week had passed in the fairy world, the countryside had changed tremendously. There were new houses and new roads all through the Glens and the old forts that he knew were gone. A hundred years and more had passed in a single week in the fairy world. As he galloped along the road, he came upon three men seeking to move a great boulder from a ditch. They did not seem to be having much success and so Ossian stopped with them to see if he could help them. Reaching down from the saddle, he put his mighty hand to the boulder to push it out. As he did so, however, the strap holding his saddle snapped and he tumbled to the ground. As soon as he hit the earth, Ossian's body crumbled to dust that blew away in the wind. Or at least most of it did for there were some remains left, which were gathered up and buried on the side of Orra Mountain. His grave marker is now no more than a few scattered stones, the remains of what was probably

some sepulchre and no-one can really say whether this is the final resting place of the great poet or not. Nevertheless, there is a tradition right across the Glens that this is where Ossian returned from the fairy world only to die in the service of others.

The Mountain also holds a tale of historical interest for it was here that the deciding battle was fought between the Norman MacQuillans and the Scottish MacDonnells which ensured MacDonnell supremacy in the area for a number of years afterwards. Known locally as 'the Battle of the Boglands', the conflict occurred in 1559 with a resounding victory for the Scotsmen. The MacQuillans had the advantage of horse and cavalry, which were led by Hugh McPhelim O'Neill and it was this which the wily MacDonnells used against them. Prior to the battle, they dug deep pits and trenches in the mountainside and covered them over with bracken and heather. The charging cavalry plunged straight into these traps and the MacDonnells cut them to pieces. Hugh McPhelim O'Neill was killed during the battle and his sepulchre lies amongst the hollows and mists around the summit of Slieveanorra.

Before reaching Cushendall and at the entrance to the Lower Glens, the road crosses the Glendun Viaduct stretching across the River Dun, known locally simply as 'the Big Bridge'. One of the major feats of engineering in the Province, the Viaduct was built between 1834 and 1839,

At the foot of the glen, Glendun Viaduct

taking the Glensmen who worked on it five summers to construct. Its architect was Charles Lanyon who had also designed some of Belfast's finest buildings, including the central buildings of Queen's University.

Cushendall itself is a quiet, restful place lying on the very edge of Red Bay. It was developed from a small coastal village in 1817 by Francis Turnley, a local landowner. Turnley had been born to wealthy parents at Richmond Lodge near Downpatrick in 1765. In 1796, he travelled to China where, through successful business interests, he amassed a fortune of £70,000. Returning to Ireland, he purchased several tracts of land, one of which contained the small village of Cushendall. Turnley decided to develop it and renamed it Newtownglens. The layout of the village is similar to that of the English Plantation towns of two hundred years earlier, based around a crossroads, which characterised the County Derry settlements of the London Guilds. The central point of the village is the Curfew Tower, situated at the very crossing of the roads. This served a dual purpose. Each of the sides of this square-shaped tower has a window on every level that looks directly down each of the four streets of the village. If there was an insurrection in the area, as was suspected there might be in the early to mid-1800s, musket men could be positioned here in order to retain control of Cushendall. The second function of the Tower was to act as the local 'lock up'. Turnley employed a pensioner named Daniel McBride, armed with a long pole

and a sword, to act as gaoler there. It is said that in all its long history, only one person was ever incarcerated in the Curfew Tower – a drunk who had become too rowdy for his own good and was held overnight in order to allow him to sober up. The Tower also housed a bell – known locally as the Curfew Bell – which, in common with the earlier Anglican towns, sounded a curfew at nine o'clock each night, a time when all decent and respectable people were supposed to be indoors. This practice continued right up until the 1940s.

In the hills behind the village and above the sea, lies the beautiful and tranquil church of Layd. Although now a ruin, this spot was once one of the burying grounds of the MacDonnells, although several other important families from the area also lie there. The little church contains something of a mystery. The sandstone building is clearly very old, dating from around 1306 and abandoned in 1790, but it seems to have been built on the site of a much older foundation. It is dedicated to St. Kieron about whom little is known. However, the holy man may have left a trail behind him which makes it possible to track his movements. Is he, for instance, the same St. Kieron who founded a monastery at Derrykeighan near Dervock, many miles away? Is he the saint who found Kilkerron (St. Kieron's Church – the original name for Campbelltown in Kintyre?). And there's another mystery concerning the building. Beneath a two storey tower lies a strange 'room',

The green glens of Antrim

the purpose of which is unknown. What was it used for? Some have suggested that it may have been a place where the priests lived but if this was the case, it must have been a very spartan existence. There's not even a place for a fire in it. Another suggestion is that it was where lepers might have gathered in order to see the Host being elevated during the Mass (the right and entitlement of every Christian person) without entering the main body of the church and spreading contagion. If this is the case, then there must have been large numbers of them for the 'room' is quite large. Its true purpose remains a perplexing mystery.

Layd churchyard lies in a V-shaped hollow of the coast with spectacular views of Scotland and the Western Isles. Some of the graves there are extremely interesting. Near the entrance, for example, is a 'holed headstone' at the top of a tall, sandstone pillar. Such headstones had legal implications in ancient Ireland. If a promissory note were passed through the hole in such a grave marker, it then had the force of Irish law behind it and, if this promise were broken, the culprit could be sued in the courts for 'breach of promise'. This was sometimes used by hill farmers around Cushendall for the buying and selling of livestock and farm produce. If the purchaser had no money, he could always pass a note through the hole as a promise of payment at some future date. It was also said to have been used by lovers to plight their troth by simply touching their fingers through the hole. This then constituted an 'engagement'.

A similar 'holed stone' can be found at the grave of the Black Nun – Julia MacQuillan – in Bonnamargy Friary at Ballycastle.

One of the more spectacular gravestones in the area – an elaborately decorated Celtic cross – is the resting place of a local medical man, Dr. James MacDonnell, who is commemorated as the founder of what was to become the forerunner for the Royal Victoria Hospital in Belfast.

Close by Cushendall are two notable geographic features. One of these, Lurigethan, is an old volcanic plug created in the days when the coastline was extremely volatile. Tracks on its slopes have also exposed white chalk amongst the basalt on its slopes which may suggest that the sea came much further inland in prehistoric times. The other is the dark and brooding shape of Tievebullagh, a peak that is rich in fairy lore. Some legends state that this mountain was once a stronghold of the Knights of the Fianna (a band of warriors in ancient Ireland) and that many mighty heroes resided there. The main thrust of the tales, however, concern the fairy kind and the mountain is said to be a bad place to traverse after dark when fairy lights can be seen gleaming from it. Geologically, the mountain is a source of a rare material called porcellanite, which was extremely valuable during prehistoric times for the manufacture of axe heads and cutting implements. Rich veins of the material are to be found in the basaltic rock, scattered along the coast as far as the White Rocks outside Portrush and it has been found in the manufacture of early axe-heads as far away as France. Indeed, many archaeologists suggest that Tievebullagh was the site of an important axe factory and may well have been one of Ireland's earliest exporting industries, linking with another axe factory on Rathlin Island.

Beyond Cushendall, the road skirts around Red Bay and continues along the coast. This was originally a military road constructed at the end of the 18th century to link the then inaccessible Glens with the important military base at Carrickfergus, further along the coast. Fears that there would be a rising in the Glens, especially after 1798, heightened the need for such a connection which has today become the Antrim Coast Road. It has followed the line of the coast, so that if necessary armies using it could be serviced directly by ships, and has in one spectacular instance been cut directly through a headland, creating a massive rock archway.

On the headland directly above this arch stand the formidable ruins of Red Bay Castle. During the mid-16th century, this fortress was the centre of MacDonnell power in the Lower Glens. It was the stronghold of James MacDonnell, second son of Alexander MacDonnell, the self-styled Lord of the Isles, based in Islay just across the water. At the height of his power and influence, James was

the 'most feared man in the North of Ireland'. The castle, built on the site of a prehistoric promontory fort, was once a fortress of the Bissets, a Scottish family who had fled from their native land following accusations of murder, to purchase 'marginal lands' (the Glens) in North Antrim. They settled in the Red Bay area and built a castle with a small settlement there. However, their relations with some of their neighbours in the Northern Glens were not especially happy. At the end of the 14th century, Eoin Bisset of Red Bay was murdered by the descendants of Sir Robert Savage of Bushmills, leaving behind only one child – his unmarried daughter Marjory.

Marjory Bisset was now heiress to much of the Glens of Antrim and as such was extremely eligible as a marriage partner. A number of the O'Neills proposed marriage but she turned them down opting instead to marry a Scotsman, John Mor MacDonnell of Islay and Kintyre. They were married in 1399 and this effectively made the Scotsman master of the Glens. Their wedding coincided with a number of bad harvests in both Kintyre and the Western Isles and, between 1400 and 1405, MacDonnell kinsmen began to arrive in the Glens looking for land. Others Scots followed and soon much of the land across the Lower Glens was Scottish owned. The MacDonnells grew in power amongst their own kind, threatening those further north and raiding along the coast as far as English-held Carrickfergus. They took over the Bisset castle and physically added to it in a more Scottish style of construction. By the mid-1500s – the time of James MacDonnell – they were the undisputed masters of the North Antrim coast and were based at Red Bay Castle.

Seeking to break their power on the northern coast, the English allied themselves with Shane O'Neill, Earl of Tyrone, supplying him with enough ships and men to launch an assault on Red Bay. O'Neill had his own score to settle with the MacDonnells as they had failed to aid him when he had earlier raised in rebellion against the English himself. Wisely he waited to attack until James MacDonnell was across in Islay, planning an invasion of the north with his elder brother Alexander. As he sailed back to the North of Ireland that night, James thought the morning had come early as the sky ahead reddened. What he was actually seeing was Red Bay Castle and its attendant village going up in flames as O'Neill's men set fire to it. Landing further along the coast, he met up with his younger brother Sorley Boy and the two of them tried to mount a defence against O'Neill's forces. They had hoped for help from the Western Isles but this was slow in coming. James and Sorley Boy were defeated by Shane O'Neill at the Battle of Glentaise on 2nd May 1565. Red Bay Castle was not rebuilt and remained a ruin on the headland. The MacDonnells were later to become the Earls of Antrim and they moved the centre of their administrative power, firstly to Dunluce and then to Glenarm further along the coast where they still maintain a castle today.

At the foot of the headland just below the ruined Castle and at the side of the road are two caves. One of these is the site of the Glens Hedge School. In Penal Times, Catholics in Ireland could not receive a formal education and even many Protestants could not afford one. Informal schools, known as 'Hedge Schools' (because many of them took place in the shadow of a hedge) were often set up in remote areas where pupils could be educated. Itinerant schoolmasters were usually employed on a daily basis. Some of them taught in the open, others in barns or outhouses but in the Glens they taught in caves. The Glens school must have been a good one as it turned out several notable scholars, including Dr. James MacDonnell who lies in Layd churchyard.

The second cave has an intriguing legend attached to it. This was said to be the home of an old lady named Anne Murray who was said to have been one of the finest distillers in the Glens. She dwelt in the cave, which she had decked out like a house – in those days (around the end of the 1700s) this was thought of as nothing unusual since a number of people lived in caves beside the sea or along rivers. Her cave opened out onto a coaching road between Carrickfergus and Cushendall, which passed directly by her door and from time to time, coaches would stop there

A walk in the Glens

so that their passengers could enjoy the results of Anne's distilling. In this way she supported herself. However it was illegal to sell home-distilled liquor and so the old lady got round this problem in a rather unusual way. At the back of her cave was a spring and so she charged the passengers a fee for a glass of water (which was not illegal) and gave them the poteen for free.

Beyond these caves lies the village of Waterfoot nestling at the mouth of Glenariff, argued by many to be the most beautiful of the glens.

Just above Waterfoot lies Glenariff Forest Park, acres of tranquil woodland with shady and pleasant walks. Deep amongst the forest glades lies a spectacular waterfall known as The Tears of the Mountain where water cascades into a deep pool. It is said that in all the Glens, this is the best place to see the fairy-kind who come and go from the pool into the landscape all around. They are often, according to local lore, best seen at evening as the light begins to soften or early in the morning as the sun comes up. This is also said to be one of the places that is special to a type of fairy, peculiar to North Antrim – the grogoch. The grogoch (sometimes spelt grugoch) is believed to be a species of leprechaun and is what might be described as a 'hairy fairy'. Completely naked, it is covered by a thick reddish fur which gathers leaves, twigs and other rubbish. Hygiene is not one of the grogoch's strong points. Indeed untidy

children are still sometimes told that they 'look like an oul' grogoch'. Despite its unkempt appearance, the grogoch is particularly friendly and is always anxious to help humans. It is extremely good-hearted and industrious but is not considered to be especially bright. It will work for almost nothing – a jug of sweet milk being the only payment it requires – and it is thought that in times gone by, many unscrupulous farmers used these fairies as a source of cheap labour. Some of the grogochs could go about invisibly – always anxious to help around the house, to the point of being a pest – causing the woman of the house to trip up or plates to be broken. Consequently grogochs were blamed for any little accidents about the house or the farmyard. They cannot abide laziness and will often climb into bed with those who lie there too long and beat them about the face in order to get them up!

One story told about the grogochs comes from Knocklayd Mountain. A shepherd had some business to transact in Ballycastle but was afraid to leave his flock in case they wandered across the Mountain and fell into holes and ravines. So he asked a friendly grogoch who lived close by if he would look after them for the day and the fairy readily agreed. The shepherd told him that he might be away overnight (although he'd try not to be) and if this happened the grogoch was simply to pen them up in a stone shelter until the morning. The grogoch told him not to worry and the shepherd went off to Ballycastle. There, he ran into

Shady waterfall, Glenariff

several friends and spent the night in the pub, drinking and making merry. In the morning, he returned to Knocklayd, fearful that the grogoch would have allowed his sheep to disperse across the mountain. To his surprise, he found the grogoch waiting for him by a rock and his sheep neatly penned in their shelter. He asked the fairy if he'd had any problems and the grogoch said that he had. All the sheep had behaved themselves except one tiny brown one, which he'd had to chase all over the mountain all night! The shepherd looked in astonishment, as he didn't possess a brown sheep. Looking into the sheepfold, he saw, lying panting in one corner, a totally exhausted hare! The silly grogoch had pursued it all across the mountain, thinking that it was a sheep!

Its position on Red Bay ensured that this was the main port of the MacDonnells and the village enjoyed some importance in the Lower Glens. Waterfoot is the gateway to Glenariff, the fertile glen and this has played a part in the development of the village. It is not, however, through farming (although that has played its part too) that Glenariff has become notable, but rather through the iron mines in the upper Glen. Fairly substantial deposits of iron ore had been detected in the basalt rock in the south-west of the Glen a number of years earlier and it was thought that there was enough to justify a major mining operation. The nearness of Waterfoot village and Red Bay made the export of ore possible and therefore added to the attractiveness of the venture. Iron mining began in Glenariff in 1873 and ended in the 1880s. Some of the entrances were no more than low tunnels cut into the rock along which men crawled in order to dig the ore out. Some were, in all probability, extremely dangerous. A small trackway led down to the village along which the raw ore could be brought down to the coast – the first three-foot gauge railway in Ireland – and traces of this can still be seen where it crossed the southern slopes of the Glen. Further back in the hills, in Glenravel (sometimes known as 'the Tenth Glen') iron mining reached a peak between the 1870s and the 1890s, with ore being transported on carts, firstly by roads and then by rail to the Bay. Together with the output of the other mines in Glenariff they were then shipped to Britain for processing and refining. The supports for a limestone-built trackway bridge, together with the remnants of an old pier and a line of miners' cottages can still be seen on the coast road out of Waterfoot on the way to Carnlough.

Besides the mines, the hills above and around the village conceal a number of other hidden sites. The first of these is the extremely ancient church of Ardclinis tucked away in a fold in the mountains. It is possible to miss this ruin on the coast road, as it is almost invisible from the lower slopes. This site dates from the earliest Christian past. No one knows who founded the church but it is clearly one of the oldest on the coast. Of particular interest is an old legend

Cottage on the coast, near Waterfoot

that the crozier of the unknown founding saint was kept in the Western window of the building and that country people, if they were accused of some crime in the area, had to come and swear their innocence upon it. If they swore falsely, their mouth was twisted, marking them as a liar for the rest of their lives. Around 1777, the crozier disappeared (some legends say that it was stolen but it is more likely to have been removed by a family named Galvin into whose care it had been given by the original saint) and was not found again until the 1920s when it was found rammed into the wall of a house in Feystown above the village of Glenarm. The woman of the house had been using it for winding wool and there was evidence that it had also been used as a pot-stirrer and, significantly, for purifying polluted wells. Realising their find, a local family placed the Ardclinis Crozier on loan to the Irish National Museum in Dublin who subsequently bought the artefact, with the proceeds going to refurbish Feystown Church. A beautiful representation of the crozier is to be found carved on the altar-screen door of the Church and, although the actual crozier is still held in Dublin, a specially-commissioned duplicate, inlaid with semi-precious stones, can be found enclosed in a glass case in the Bay Chapel in Waterfoot.

The fact that the crozier was actually held at the church suggests that it may well have had some association with the Culdee sect of 9th and 10th century Ireland. This was a mysterious and austere order of Irish monks into whose care many of the staffs of the early saints had been given. Perhaps one of them founded Ardclinis Church – the nearness of trees and of running water (central to the Culdee view of nature) might suggest this. From Ardclinis, the Culdees might have travelled to the West of Scotland and into the Western Isles, where they founded a number of churches. Whoever built it, the church was a ruin by the mid-1500s, its limestone stonework not withstanding the harsh sea winds which blew in from Scotland. However, the attendant graveyard contains a number of important tombs including those dedicated to the O'Neills.

The other secluded site is the near-abandoned village of Galboly, hidden deep amongst the coastal mountains, well back from the road. This is sometimes called 'the Hidden Village' and was most probably a *clachan* – a village used by herdsmen and their families when the moved their herds and flocks to higher pasture. The name means either 'the bright dairying place' or 'the dairying place of the stranger' and at one time the village was a stop on the coaching route along the coast. However the road up into Galboly was so steep that oxen had to be attached to pull the horses up to it. The village was incredibly remote and, according to tradition, because there was no law there, it was the perfect place for highwaymen who plundered coaches and robbed travellers on the lower roads. A shebeen operated there, owned by a man named Murphy, but run by a woman called Mary Leckey. The shebeen was the headquarters for ruthless robbers and thieves who terrorised and murdered throughout the whole district. In the 1960s, whilst lifting a limestone slab, workmen discovered several skeletons laid out in a row underneath – all victims of the Galboly highwaymen. The drinking house finally closed its doors around 1845 with a party which lasted for three days.

Family ties in the village were very strong – women who married outside the area were not required to take their husbands' surnames and were known by their maiden names. This was not unusual in some remote areas. People who lived in the Upper village were not allowed to buy property in the Lower village and in this way the various families kept control of their lands.

Galboly was finally more or less abandoned in the 1960s. By this time the number of people living there had dwindled and many of the families went to live in nearby Carnlough. By the time it was deserted, many of the buildings in the single street were already in ruins. Today only one building is habitable – this was the last to be abandoned. The views from Galboly to the Mull of Kintyre and the Scottish coast are breathtaking and the mountains round about are full of wild flowers and heathers. Just beyond the Hidden Village, the land rises into a scree down which gravel and rocks slide year after year with the heavy rains that come and go over the highlands. Who knows

for how much longer secret places such as Galboly, hidden away among the hills, can survive?

Heading home, near Garron Point

The Lower Glens and the Plateau

—: Tales of Saints and Sinners :—

On the road which runs along the coast, between Glenariff and Glenarm, stands a tall chalk pillar which was once a sea-stack and which is known locally as the White Lady. It has the appearance of a stately, bustled Victorian woman and a little further along is another column, which resembles a bowed Irish woman, her head covered with a shawl. These two pillars are connected in legend. It is said that the White Lady was once a human who was actually of relatively low birth but gave herself airs and graces above her station. She dressed only in the finest clothes and went about in a haughty manner. Her old mother who was a simple soul, had to work extremely hard in order to afford the grand finery and ornaments for her daughter. At last the daughter's demands became so extravagant and expensive that the old woman was forced to work on the Sabbath in order to raise the money. Angered, both by the old woman's blasphemy and the daughter's haughtiness, God turned them both to stone as a warning to those who would act extravagantly or work on the sacred day!

A short distance further on, near Garron Point is another stone with a more historical significance. It is a large and inscribed piece of chalk, which has been raised to the memory of those from the area who died in the Great Potato Famine which raged in Ireland between 1845 and 1852. The Famine was particularly bad in the Glens, with hunger and disease rampant, and there are many stories about those who simply died from starvation or from eating poisoned shellfish.

Garron Point itself – the name means 'neck of the horse'

– is a long spar of land, stretching out into the sea like the neck of the animal from which it takes its name. Here stands Garron Tower House – now a Catholic college – but originally built by Frances Anne Vane, Lady Londonderry. In order to create the extensive grounds around the house, Lady Londonderry demolished two small villages – One and a Half Acres (demolished to create a gate lodge) and Dunmaul (the ruins of which now form the back of the College). Both of these were principal villages on the main coaching route from Carrickfergus and the Lady closed off this road and created a special route for her own carriages. The Tower became something of a summer retreat and is famous for an elaborately carved door (still in existence), which led into the main ballroom of the house.

The small town of Carnlough, nestling at the foot of Glencloy (the Glen of the hedges) was once owned by Lady Londonderry's grandson, Sir Winston Churchill, then Secretary of State for War, whose picture still hangs in the town's main hotel – the Londonderry Arms. Carnlough originally started out around the 17th century, as a small fishing village but has now developed into an attractive seaside town with its picturesque harbour and limestone arch. The town also boasts the smallest townland in Ireland – the townland of Mill Tenement, which, as its name suggests was once no more than a tenement for mill-workers. Now is is a single building which was formerly a shop, along the town's Waterfall Road.

Beyond Carnlough lies the small village of Glenarm which is probably the only village in Ireland (or indeed in the United Kingdom) to boast a municipal charter, entitling it to become a Borough. This charter was said to have been granted by King John sometime in the early 13th century. Although a tranquil and quiet place, Glenarm (one of the oldest towns in Ireland) was once a centre of industry, with extensive fishing and trading being carried on from its 15th century harbour. Following the fall of Dunluce Castle, Glenarm became the principal residence of the Earls of Antrim, remaining so for over four hundred years, and the present Earl, Randal MacDonnell (the 15th Earl of Antrim), still officially resides there today. A major feature of the village is the magnificent Barbican Gate to Glenarm Castle, built by Edmund MacDonnell when he restored the building in 1825.

The present Castle itself dates from 1936 although the history of a fortification at Glenarm dates from around the late 13th/early 14th century. The original castle was once a stronghold of the Bissets who held much of the Lower Glens before the coming of the MacDonnells. It was attacked and burned during the wars along the coast but was rebuilt by Randal MacDonnell in 1636, this time on the north side of the Glenarm River. Six years later, it was attacked and burned again and left as a ruin. However, it was rebuilt in 1750 and was briefly used as a barracks for local yeomanry and Scottish officers during the Rebellion of 1798.

Sailing out of Carnlough

Light on the water, Glenarm Castle

Today the town is still the centre for salmon and lobster fisheries, which work closely inshore in Glenarm Bay near the village. Glenarm salmon is to be found on the menus of many up-market restaurants all across Northern Ireland and the lobsters are exported all across Europe.

Climbing up into the East Antrim Plateau, the coastline soon falls away behind. Above Glenarm and near the edge of the mountain road, lies an extremely ancient churchyard bordering on the Earl of Antrim's estate. The old place has a very violent history. During the Rebellion of the United Irishmen in 1798, a number of suspected rebels were held by the local yeomanry in Glenarm Castle, including the local Presbyterian minister who was suspected of being one of the rebel leaders. In retaliation, a number of the rebels seized the families of local yeomen and brought them to the old cemetery where they threatened to kill them unless the prisoners were released. Faced with such a deadly proposal, the guards in Glenarm Castle had no other option but to release the prisoners, pleading with the local clergyman to intercede on their families' behalf. Setting aside his clerical collar, however, he immediately donned an officer's uniform and ordered all the prisoners in the churchyard to be shot unless the garrison in the Castle surrendered. The garrison refused to do so and the situation had now become so desperate that another Presbyterian clergyman from Larne had to be brought in to negotiate the release of the captives. As the Rebellion in the Glens crumbled, the Presbyterian clergyman in Glenarm put his soldier's uniform aside and took up his pulpit once more. What eventually became of him thereafter is unknown. The old cemetery where the hostages were held still remains, however, and although it is now cleaned up, it was once an overgrown and extremely spooky place.

The mountain road that runs between Glenarm and Broughshane is an incredibly lonely one and was once reputedly the haunt of highwaymen who attacked lone travellers. One of the most famous of these during the early 18th century, was Captain Jack McAllister, a brutal thug who allegedly came from Buckna and who headed a murderous gang of robbers and cut throats. Although not strictly a 'Captain', he assumed the title to give himself both status and credibility in the surrounding lands. McAllister is reputedly the only man to have escaped three times from Carrickfergus Castle where he was held awaiting trial. On the last occasion, he was allegedly recaptured and hanged in front of the Castle itself without benefit of law. His gang was taken over by Naoise (or Ness) O'Haughan, one of an outlaw family who came from Glenwhirrey, near Ballymena, and who terrorised the lands as far as Antrim town for a good many years. However, Jack McAllister is said to have left a fabulous treasure – loot from his various robberies – hidden somewhere amongst the mountains. And there is a clue: go to a place where you can see seven stretches of water, all in the county of Antrim; this is where the treasure is buried

Evening catch, Glenarm Bay

under a thorn bush. In some versions of the story, part of the fortune was found by a schoolmaster who located it at a place called the Hanging Thorn in the area of Carnstroan. However, other locations for the hoard are given at a place called Archie's Bushes, which is somewhere in the King's Moss outside Antrim and in a region close to the Braid Sheddings between Glenarm and Broughshane.

The lonely mountains, with their deep caves and ravines were once the ideal hiding places for highwaymen and legends of them remain throughout the area. In Glenariff, for instance, a highway robber is said to be buried, together with yet another fabulous hoard, under a big stone, which legend dictates cannot be lifted.

The seams of iron ore which were evident around Glenariff are to be found in this mountainous area as well, and at one time these uplands were also the centre of a fairly intensive mining industry. The first mining development started in the 1830s under Nicholas Crommelin who began to extract crude iron ore and smelt it using a peat furnace. The ruins of this furnace can still be seen on the edge of the small mining town, which Crommelin founded – Newtowncrommelin. However, it was James Fisher, a mining developer from Barrow-in-Furness who began to mine the area in earnest in 1866. Leasing land on a yearly basis and at a cost of £10 per annum from the local landowner, Edward Benn, he opened ore mines on the slopes of Slievearee. He founded the mining settlement of Fishertown, which has now reverted to its old Irish name of Cargan, meaning a small, rocky place. Fisher's efforts proved successful and by 1873, the mines were producing 18,000 tons of iron ore, which was shipped to Red Bay by horse and cart with over 700 men being employed in the mines themselves. A small railway was set up but was attacked and sabotaged by the hauliers who saw it as undermining their livelihood. A railway also ran between Ballymena and the top of Parkmore and was opened in 1875. The last train ran along this line in 1937. By this time, the village and the mines were more or less gone although there was some mining for bauxite (a constituent of aluminium) during the War – this continued up until 1945 when the last mine closed.

The tiny village of Martinstown set in Glenravel (the Glen of the Berries – often referred to as 'the tenth Glen') completes the three villages of this area. It is said that, early in his ministry in Ireland, Saint Patrick came here, asking for buttermilk, and was refused by local people who said that there was none to be had in the entire locality. In response, the saint struck the side of a nearby mountain with his crozier and buttermilk issued forth. Patrick now declared that the people of Glenravel would never more want for buttermilk. Today, the area is prosperous farming country.

The post office, Newtowncrommelin

In the late 19th century, the Glen was the centre of the mining industry, with many locals employed in both the iron and bauxite mines. Today, with the mines long closed, Martinstown is a stop on the road from Ballymena to Cushendall.

High up, on the very edge of the Glens, lies the hill settlement of Clogh. The name 'Clogh' simply means stone and it is thought that this was the site of an ancient standing stone which was venerated in the locality – great standing stones are still very much in evidence throughout the countryside here. At one stage, according to Ordnance Survey records, there may have been a convent or nunnery somewhere in this area. The village is built on the remains of an ancient hill fort, which once guarded an important pass that led through the hills from the coast to the boggy lowlands outside present-day Ballymena. Indeed, so important was it that the MacQuillans of Dunluce raised a castle there to guard the pass and to levy a toll from travellers coming through the hills. It was here that part of Shane O'Neill's army was said to have camped on their way back from burning the MacDonnell castle at Red Bay. Clogh Castle was later held by the Stewarts of Ballintoy as part of the Earl of Antrim's estate, but was captured by rebels during the 1642 Rebellion. It was finally destroyed in the 1650s by Cromwellian troops from Carrickfergus, although the ruins are still to be seen on the edge of the village. The half-ruined tower has been locally nicknamed

Summer shadows, Cottage in the Glens

'The Lug o' the Tub' – a handle by which a tub is lifted – and has given its name to the local hostelry.

Clogh was once an important post town and boasted a change-house and a major inn in its centre. Here, coach passengers could alight whilst the horses rested, and sample the delights of the village including, it is believed, the local poteen. From Clogh, the coaching road led through the hills towards Loughguile and here local highwaymen – many, apparently, bearing the surname 'O'Hara' – were particularly active. So much so, in fact, that many coach-drivers refused to go there, preferring to travel the lower roads across the Garry Bog instead.

On the lower slopes below Clogh village stands Dunbought Fort. Like Clogh itself, this is an extremely ancient site and from it, a number of other forts and tree-clumps can be seen stretching all across the Garry Bog. It is thought that the Fort was one of the principal sites on a prehistoric trading road across the hills and that the other sites mark 'signposts' on a route across the treacherous Bog below in the days before maps. Recently, a number of old stone fortress walls have been discovered at Dunbought, perhaps marking it as an important defensive site.

The Garry Bog itself is a large stretch of marshland, which stretches across the lands north of Ballymena towards Ballymoney, running almost parallel with the Plateau.

Although parts of it were considered to be extremely treacherous, a number of coaching roads still ran through it. These were used by coachmen coming from Belfast who had no wish to try the upper roads across the East Antrim Plateau which were plagued with highwaymen. The Bog was cut by a number of small but fast-flowing rivers, the most dangerous of which was the Clogh River. There were two principal crossings on this river – one at Glarryford (the name simply means 'the muddy crossing') and the other at Dundermot. The Ordnance Survey Memoirs state that the best crossing was at Glarryford as the bridge at Dundermot was in a poor state of repair, and not suitable for some coaches.

The mound of Dundermot stands a little way from the main Ballymena-Ballymoney carriageway and close to the road that runs down into Glarryford. It is a rather sinister-looking place, overgrown with trees and twisted roots. In ancient times, it was believed to be a gateway to Hell or some sort of fairy mound, which, on both May Eve and Hallowe'en opened to let loose the supernatural forces of the Otherworld. Anybody in the general vicinity could be carried away, never to be seen again. There is the story of a coach which vanished into this hill as the driver tried to reach Coleraine in the middle of a ferocious downpour. From time to time, the ghost vehicle is reputedly seen in the locality and its presence always signals the death of those who see it. These are, of course, only old legends

Cattle grazing, Garry Bog

– Dundermot was probably no more than one of a line of motte and bailey fortifications, raised by the Normans and stretching between Ballycastle and Antrim town. Other such mounds exist all through the area, to the outskirts of Ballymena. They may have been used as staging posts for Norman forces travelling through the region or to subdue the surrounding district. However, such places were usually regarded with great suspicion and fear by the Irish and were usually best avoided.

During the late 17th century, the nearby village of Glarryford was once the home of one of the most ferocious bounty hunters in the whole of Antrim. This was John Johnston who hunted down highwaymen for the Antrim Assizes. There were a number of such men scattered all across the North and they were known as 'Tory-hunters' (the term 'Tory' coming from an old Irish word meaning, 'outlaw'). Of all the Tory-hunters in Ulster, Johnston was one of the most successful, tracking down and decapitating (the bounty was paid on the head of a highwayman presented at a local military barracks) a large number of highway robbers. There are still Johnstons living in the village today who may well be his descendants.

Today, a main road leads straight across the Bog replacing the old coaching tracks which formerly wound their way through it. This partly follows the line of a road, which was laid by the architect Charles Lanyon (who also designed the Glendun Viaduct). Built in 1840, the road put into practice Lanyon's novel plans for building a stable road across an uncertain quagmire. This involved planting, over the deepest part of the Bog, a decorative avenue of fifty hardy Scots pine whose roots would help support the roadway. The group of trees, known as The Frosses (the name, which literally means 'showers', signifies a deep or watery place) proved a success story and gave their name to the main road between Ballymena and Ballymoney. Several of them can still be seen today although the majority of Lanyon's plantation have long since been removed, some only very recently.

In the south of the East Antrim Plateau stands one of Northern Ireland's best-known peaks – Slemish Mountain. This holy mountain has strong connections with St. Patrick – the Patron Saint of Ireland – as, according to legend, the saint tended pigs on its lower slopes in his early days.

Nearby, on the summit of a small conical hill stand the ruins of a medieval church, which is said to stand on the site of the first church raised by St. Patrick in Ireland. Indeed, according to legend, the site is far older since this was the fortress of Milchu, Lord of the Wastes of *Slabh Mis* (Slemish), the master who bought Patrick into slavery from the Irish pirates who had captured him. Patrick escaped and fled to the Continent where he was reputedly baptised as a Bishop before returning to Ireland. Hearing that he had

Solitude, Skerry Church

returned with the authority of God, Milchu committed suicide by burning his fortress. His son, however, accepted Christianity and donated the area of land to Patrick to build his church. It was here that the saint is said to have received a vision from God. The angel Victor appeared to him and gave the saint a marvellous crozier known as the Beculam Jesu and also details of his mission in Ireland. There is still a footprint etched in the rock, which is said to be that of the angel. The church-site is probably a very old inauguration site for local kings and warlords. The view from the summit of this hill extends all the way as far as Antrim and such high places were often used so that a chieftain could survey his entire kingdom as he was being inaugurated. The footprint, cut into the rock, was perhaps where he placed his right foot in order to show his 'oneness' with the earth over which he ruled. This was probably an important pagan site, long before the coming of the Christian Church.

The ruined medieval church that now stands on the site may have been an ancient penitential church. Penitential churches were awarded the distinction of being able to perform a special Mass which could forgive any sin, provided the supplicant was truly penitent. They were usually situated in remote and difficult places so that the mere act of getting to them was an act of penitence in itself. The Skerry Church, as the place is known locally, is certainly hard to approach over stony and gorse-covered fields and so it is quite possible that such Masses were said

there. The ruin boasts a fairly extensive burying ground that includes some tombs of the O'Neills who were masters of the area around Broughshane. Somewhere in this locality too, is said to be the well where St. Patrick was baptised into the Christian Church, whilst still a slave, by the faceless monk Geronius, though its location appears to have been lost.

From the ruined church it is possible to look across right into Slemish. The mountain is actually a large volcanic plug – part of the same volcanic activity that pushed up the East Antrim highlands and is probably one of the biggest such plugs in Ireland. A small track runs right the way up to the summit and in summer, pilgrims sometimes make the climb in memory of St. Patrick, usually on the 17th March which is the saint's Feast Day. The area all around is dotted with dry stonewalls which have been put together by craftsmen. This art of building a permanent wall without the aid of mortar or cement is a skill which was once common all through the Glens and beyond but is now in grave danger of dying out completely. However, there are still many examples to be found in the hills between Glenarm and Ballymena.

Beyond Slemish, the mountainous land falls away to the fertile valley of the River Braid and the villages, clustered around the important valley town of Ballymena.

Curiosity, Farmland near Slemish

Winter reflections, Braid River

Around Ballymena

—: Tales of Devils and Doctors :—

Early accounts of Ballymena simply describe it as a *dirty, straggling village on the road to Broughshane'*. In actual fact, Ballymena is largely comprised of two villages – Ballymena and Harryville (now a suburb of the greater Ballymena area). The name 'Ballymena' is generally taken to mean 'the middle town' (i.e. it is in the middle of County Antrim) but it more probably means 'the town of the monks'. Given its close proximity to the holy mountain of Slemish, associated with St. Patrick, it is quite possible that there was a major monastery there in an early time.

The town is surrounded by small villages, one of which is Broughshane. This was an area of ancient earthworks and standing stones, denoting a history, which stretched back to Mesolithic times. The village takes its name from ancient fort (called a 'brock' in the Scottish tongue) belonging to Shane McBrien O'Neill, who also built Shane's Castle on the shores of Lough Neagh. This was Shane's Brock – although the fort may have been far older than the family that owned it – and these were O'Neill lands, which were extensively planted after the Flight of the Earls. Presbyterians flooded in, taking lands along the River Braid, laying the foundations for the spinning and weaving industries which would come into their own in the 18th and 19th centuries. Broughshane would become a foremost linen village and its people would become prosperous. A number of large mills were built and one of these, Houston's Mill, formerly owned by the Houston family, can still be seen today in the centre of the village, testifying to Broughshane's importance at the time. The rich farming

Bluebell wood near Broughshane

land that surrounded the village – part of the fertile Braid Valley – ensured that even with the linen slump of the mid-19th century, that the area remained relatively prosperous. Dominated by St. Patrick's Anglican Church, the village is still an attractive, colourful place, having won many awards for its tidiness and floral displays.

Another village in the area is Galgorm, now the headquarters of the local educational authority. The main feature of the village is an ancient castle, the site of which dates back to the time of the MacQuillans. Following the Battle of Orra Beg Mountain, the castle passed into the hands of Colla MacDonnell, younger brother of James MacDonnell of Red Bay, who did extensive restructuring work to it, turning it into a 'Scottish style' fortress. Shortly after the Plantation of Ulster, however, Galgorm Castle received its most famous occupant – the alleged warlock, Doctor Alexander Colville. At this time, the name of the village was changed to Mount Colville.

Doctor Colville was a Doctor of Divinity. He was also a High Anglican and this did not sit easily with the people round about, many of whom were his tenants and staunch Presbyterians. The Doctor's high-handed manner and total disdain for the Presbyterian faith did not endear him to them in any way either. He was also initially very wealthy, though nobody was sure as to the source of his fortune. A rumour went around the area that he was a wizard and

that in Galgorm Castle was a library filled with diabolical books. Using one of these blasphemous tomes, Dr. Colville is alleged to have summoned up the Devil, during a time of personal financial crisis, and is said to have sold his soul to the Evil One. The payment was to be made in two stages, the first being to fill an old top boot (long-legged riding boot), which stood in the kitchens of Galgorm, right up to the brim, with gold. This, the Devil began to do, but found to his amazement that the gold just kept pouring into the boot. The crafty Doctor had removed the heel from the boot and had placed it over a hole that led directly to the Castle cellars and so the Devil actually had to fill the cellars as well. The second payment was simply to fill an old soft hat, belonging to the Doctor, with gold. This time the Devil, wisely, did not meet Colville in Galgorm Castle but beside an old limekiln on the road to Broughshane. The Doctor held out the hat over the kiln and the Devil began to fill it with gold. However, Doctor Colviille had made a slit in the crown and so the gold filled up the limekiln as well. The Devil departed with a curse, stating that he would come to collect the Doctor's soul in thirteen years time.

Doctor Colville, says the legend, now began to make preparations for that event. He prayed, he sang psalms and when the Devil came for him (traditionally held to be on the 28th February, which was the time that they'd agreed), he found the cleric in the old church beside the

Castle, reading his Bible by the light of a candle. The Devil, of course, could not approach a man when God's Word is open and so Doctor Colville asked if he might continue reading until the candle had burned down. When the Devil agreed, the Doctor promptly snuffed it out and placed it in the Bible (where the Devil couldn't reach it) declaring that it would never be snuffed out. His triumph over the Devil was, however, short-lived. Later, in the darker months of the year, and whilst the Doctor was away in Belfast, an old servant was doing some work in Galgorm Castle and needed a little light. Looking in the old Bible, she found the scrap of candle and lit it, allowing it to burn down. As soon as the flame had consumed the last piece of wax, a peal of diabolical laughter rang through Galgorm Castle and upon his return Doctor Colville turned deathly pale. He dismissed the old servant and began to hatch a plan to save his soul. As the date on which the Devil had agreed to collect his soul was at the end of February, the Doctor made sure that around that date he was always praying, reading his Bible or singing hymns in which case the Devil could not approach him. However, as soon as the 1st March dawned, he was back to his old ways, drinking and carousing with his friends and tormenting his tenants.

One evening at the end of February, he had been seemingly particularly pious, spending most of the day in prayer and religious reflection. As twelve o'clock tolled, he quickly reverted to his drinking and loose behaviour, declaring that this was 'the best 1st March that he'd enjoyed in a long time'. One of his guests, however, who possessed an almanac, pointed out that it was not the 1st March at all but the 29th February – the year was a Leap Year. At this, the Doctor turned deathly pale and tried to find his Bible. It was too late for there was a thunderous knock at the doors of Galgorm Castle and as an old servant went to answer, they burst open to admit the Devil in the guise of a tall dark man wearing a green travelling cloak. This he threw around the Doctor and they both disappeared in a puff of sulphurous smoke, presumably to Hell.

This is the legend which is extremely well known in the area. There is no doubt that Doctor Alexander Colville existed as his portrait hangs in the hallway of Galgorm Castle. Tradition says that if the picture is removed, then the Castle itself will fall and a terrible pestilence will come upon Galgorm village. There are other stories about the Castle as well – that the Devil still prowls about the grounds in the shape of a huge, black dog with red eyes or that Doctor Colville's ghost is frequently seen in the Castle gardens (which he created), consulting an old sundial at the very centre of the walkways. The ancient church in which the Doctor is supposed to have met the Devil is still there, with a mysterious and sinister-looking tomb under the alter where Doctor Colville is said to lie (presumably his body wasn't actually carried off by the Devil) encased in

Summer light, Galgorm Castle

a brass coffin. Few local people will willingly venture into the tomb, especially after dark! The stories may be nothing more than tales born out of animosities between Alexander Colville and his tenants, and the Doctor's high-handedness towards his Presbyterian neighbours' faith. For instance, he was summoned to explain himself before a Presbyterian Conference in Belfast but ignored the summons and went fishing instead. He was allegedly seen, sitting on the banks of the Braid, surrounded by demons and fairies – doubtless an exaggeration put about by his neighbours. The name of the 'Devil Doctor', however, has given Galgorm a slightly sinister reputation all across Antrim.

Interestingly, the Castle was later used, in 1690, as a headquarters, by the Williamite General, the Duke of Wurtemburg who quartered his men there, most of whom seem to have been either German or Danish. This might explain some old Danish coinage which had been found in some of the bogs round about.

Near Ballymena too is the picturesque village of Kells nestling close to the Kellswater. This has a long and religious history. In early Christian Ireland, there seems to have been some sort of cell or hermitage, perhaps occupied by a solitary monk or hermit, somewhere close to the present village. A church together with a Celtic monastery seems to have been founded in the area of Templemoyle, the date of which is given as being around 480. This was

attacked and burned by the Vikings who devastated the mid-Antrim area in 831. According to the Ordnance Survey Memoirs, this foundation was rebuilt and extended in the latter part of the 9th century by a chieftain or holy man named O'Brien Carragh, who founded a much larger religious house there. This became a significant monastic foundation that existed up until the 15th century and may well have been administratively important in the area since the neighbouring area of Connor has given its name to the ecclesiastical diocese of Down and Connor. Following the Plantation of Ulster, the area was extensively settled by Presbyterians who removed many traces of the 'Romish' religious foundation. Today, little trace of this holy house remains.

Kells was also said to be the home of another famous highwayman, Robert Archer. Archer was hanged in Ballymena at the end of the 18th century and his body reputedly swung on the gallows for months as there was no one to cut him down. Tales of his exploits, either real or imaginary have formed the basis of local folklore for years. The most common story about him was that he was betrayed to the authorities by a school-friend that he used to visit. This gentleman informed the local authorities that when Archer was next visiting, he (the friend) would send a boy down to buy a wheaten bannock and thus the authorities would be alerted. This was done and Archer was found asleep at his erstwhile friend's house and was arrested.

River path in Autumn, Kellswater

The story is not native to the region as it is to be found in several parts of Scotland, relating to several highwaymen there – it is even connected with the great Scottish hero, William Wallace, who was said to have been similarly betrayed by Sir John Monteith. However, the daring exploits of Robert Archer appear undiminished by this.

Another village, Ahoghill, lies not far away on the road to Portglenone. The name may come from Magherahoghill, which means plain of the ford of the yew wood that may have at one time denoted an important river crossing. This may well have been the main crossing between two now vanished petty kingdoms or territories within the mid-Antrim area or it may have been a significant military crossing used by various armies. Excavations in the landscape round about have shown that this region was the scene of many ancient battles, some of them dating back to earliest times, showing that the ford was in use even then and that the surrounding area was extremely warlike. The river crossing may also have been on a trading route and may well have been used by merchants coming from the coast. In 1688, tradition states that the army of James II crossed there on their way to Portglenone and the Siege of Derry. The importance of the village was emphasised in 1970 when a former Prime Minister of Northern Ireland, Captain Terence O'Neill (Prime Minister from March 1963 until May 1969) was elevated to the English Peerage. He chose as his title, Baron O'Neill of the Main

in Ahoghill in the County of Antrim, thus giving the village an aristocratic status. Ahoghill is sometimes linked ecclesiastically with Portglenone and it is possible that there was some sort of holy house there at one time, linked with a monastery which existed in the South Derry village and which is still there today. Ahogill formed a massive ecclesiastical parish in the Antrim midlands, part of which can still be traced.

This mid-Antrim area is famous for its connections with several Presidents of the United States of America. The ancestors of President William McKinley (1897-1901), for example, came from Conaghel, near Ballymoney, whilst the forebears of President Andrew Jackson (1829-1837) came from outside Carrickfergus. However, the village of Cullybackey can claim a direct connection with the parents of President Chester Alan Arthur (1881-1885). The low thatched house in which his father and mother lived still exists today, pretty much as it was in the early 19th century, and is now an interpretive centre. Like many of the other villages round about, Cullybackey was a centre of the linen industry. The name, however, has become so Anglicised as to render its meaning obscure, although there have been several suggestions as to its origin. For instance, it may well mean 'the wood of the birches' or another explanation may be 'the corner of the spades', as there is a suggestion that there may have been an establishment there for making the blades of wooden spades.

The village was extensively settled by Presbyterians engaged in the linen industry and one of its central features is the Cunningham Memorial Presbyterian Church, which was built in 1880 using donations provided by the Misses Cunningham of Ardvernis in memory of their mother. In 1905 Miss Jane Cunningham made a number of improvements to the church including the installation of electricity.

In the 19th century, Cullybackey was no more than a single street, although a recent expansion of the village (largely an overflow from neighbouring Ballymena and from Belfast) have greatly extended it. Even so, at one time, Cullybackey boasted a racecourse, which was frowned upon by local Presbyterians. Eventually, and under local pressure, it was sold off and became a golf club, although nowadays the location has changed.

All these villages – mainly formed during the linen heyday in the Braid Valley – cluster round the central town of Ballymena. Founded on, or close to, the site of an old monastery, the town – certainly one of the most prosperous in mid-Antrim – has developed out of two villages which have come together to form the present Borough. Of the two of them, Ballymena is certainly the older. Relics such as arrowheads and brooch clasps dating back thousands of years have been found around the town, suggesting extremely early settlement in the area.

Lighting the past, Arthur Cottage

Between the years 900 and 1100, the area was invaded by the O'Flynns who had fortresses along the North Antrim coast (one of the most significant being Dunluce) who repelled the Normans in the Antrim midlands, around the beginning of the 12th century. They would hold a precarious position there until around 1300, when they were ousted by an expansion of a clan of the O'Neills known as the *Clanna Bui* (the yellow clan, because they mainly had fair hair and who gave their name to Clandeboy) and fled south towards Ards. The O'Neills now controlled the area and they supported the Scottish contender, Edward Bruce (younger brother of the more famous Robert) when he was crowned King of Ireland at Carrickfergus in 1315. They further supported him when he battled the Norman Richard de Burgo, Red Earl of Ulster, at Tannybrake (Tawnybrak), five miles south of present-day Ballymena, near Kells. The Earl was defeated and was forced to flee to Coleraine with Bruce's army in pursuit. By 1318, however, Bruce had been killed at Faughart, near Drogheda and the O'Neills found themselves defending their lands against the invigorated Normans. This was to usher in over a century of conflict as the English tried to gain a foothold in the area.

In 1576, following the major rebellion of Shane O'Neill, Queen Elizabeth I seized the mid-Antrim lands and handed them to Sir Thomas Smith, an 'undertaker' who undertook to drive off the indigenous Irish, plant the lands and make them loyal to the English Crown. His settlement was to fail and by 1581, the Ballymena area had been taken back into ownership of the English Crown. An Inquisition of the new English king, James I, set up in 1605, divided the lands of North Clandeboy (in which Ballymena lay), placing the site of the town in the district of Clanarghty, part of the parish of Ahoghill and in 1607, James handed the lands to Rory Og McQuillan, who claimed it as a reinstatement of his ancient entitlement. His ownership of the lands, however, was not to last very long.

The 'Ballymenoch Estate' now passed through a number of owners until it came into the hands of William Adair, a landlord from Kinhilt in southwest Scotland. The name of the small settlement on these lands temporarily changed its name from 'Ballymenoch' to 'Kinhiltstown' in honour of its owner's Scottish lands. However by 1669, it had changed its name back once more and it is recorded that there were approximately 106 houses on the Estate. This was quite a sizeable settlement for the time.

Early in the 1600s, a castle had been built in Ballymena, taking advantage of an ancient fort, which stood on the banks of the River Braid (at the southern end of Castle Street today) and this probably formed the nucleus for the expanding town. Around 1624, King Charles I granted permission for William Adair to hold a market there every Saturday, an indication of the growing importance of the town and its fortification. In fact in 1641, during the Irish Rebellion, it was besieged by rebels from the Glens and although the garrison there held out for a time, they were forced to retreat to Carrickfergus. The rebels then moved on to besiege Clogh Castle in the East Antrim hills and the Adairs returned to reclaim their lands. They rebuilt parts of the town which had been destroyed in the Rebellion and in 1654 a Market House was built and was fully operational.

By 1690, the village was well established and, during the Williamite Wars in Ireland, the major landlord, Sir Robert Adair, a staunch supporter of William III, raised a Regiment of Foot from the Ballymena district, which later fought at the Battle of the Boyne.

The village of Ballymena continued to grow and expand and by 1704, there was a population of well over 800 living there, making it virtually a small town by the standards of the day. And it continued to grow, aided by the linen industry in the surrounding area, so that by 1783 it was one of nine of the foremost towns in the North of Ireland, specialising in the manufacture of brown linen.

During the Rebellion of 1798, which was largely Presbyterian-led, Ballymena was occupied by over 10,000 United Irishmen who stormed the Market House (which stood on the site of what is now the Town Hall) and managed to temporarily hold the town against troops from

Ballymena Town Hall

nearby Antrim. They eventually surrendered, following the failure of the Rebellion and many of them were arrested and executed. Despite the unsettled times, Ballymena kept on expanding.

In 1831, a market was built at the Fair Hill by William Adair and rapidly became the foremost trading centre in the area. It was followed in 1865 by the building of a new castle (the original one having completely burnt down in 1740), a magnificent residence for the Adair family, surrounded by an extensive Demesne. It was, however, not finally completed until 1887 but would survive until the 1950s when it was finally pulled down to make way for a housing estate. Around the castle, Ballymena continued to develop. It was aided by the fact that in 1848 a railway link between the town and Belfast had been established. This connection would eventually be extended to Coleraine and to the holiday destination of Portrush. Taking advantage of this important railway link in 1866, a group of local businessmen set up the Braidwater Spinning Company, which was to become a major employer in the area and was only finally demolished in 1998 to make way for the Braidwater Retail Park. Its tower was one of the 'landmark sights' of Ballymena.

The town has often been referred to as 'The City of the Seven Towers' and this nickname came about in the late 1800s when Sir Robert Alexander Shafto Adair (the 1st Lord Waveney) identified the seven most famous landmarks in Ballymena. These were the tower of the Old Parish Church; the tower of the Church of Ireland; the tower of Ballymena First Presbyterian Church; the tower of All Saints Roman Catholic Church; the tower on the old Town Hall; the tower of the Braidwater Spinning Mill and the central tower of Ballymena Castle. Sadly, only three of those towers still exist today – All Saints Roman Catholic Church, St. Patrick's Church of Ireland and the Old Parish Church. Although technically not a 'city', Ballymena is nevertheless still one of the most prosperous towns in mid-Antrim.

The history of Harryville (now a suburb of Ballymena) is much more recent. It was founded by (and named after) Henry Hutchinson Hamilton O'Hara (1829-1875), an eccentric local landlord who built the village for some of his tenants. The O'Haras were an old Gaelic family whose roots went back to the times before the Plantation and who owned a large area of land, which stretched from Portstewart on the North Derry coast, through Loughguile (where they had a major castle) to the Braid River. Henry Hutchinson Hamilton owned a castle at Crebilly (just above present-day Ballymena town) and was by far the strangest of them all. He was affectionately known as 'the Fool O'Hara' in the locality and many stories about him have passed into local folklore.

Standing fast, Ballymena's remaining towers

The most common tale about him concerns his marriages. Henry lived at Crebilly with his invalided mother and, during the 1840s, in order to lift her health and to escape the worst effects of the Potato Famine (which had hit the area quite hard), he took her on holiday to France. There he interviewed a companion for her (the lady's name is often given as Madeline) and brought her home to attend to his mother and live with the family at Crebilly. Soon after his return, he married her in the nearby Catholic chapel. Things were blissfully happy for a year or so and in a fit of generosity, the Squire O'Hara bought a house in London for Madeline's parents and instructed her to go over and help them settle in. Whilst she was away, he married again to a Protestant lady of the countryside to whom he'd been attracted before going to France. He declared that his first marriage had 'not been lawful' as it had been conducted by a Catholic priest. This satisfied his Presbyterian tenants who had not taken to the Catholic Madeline at all. However, his second wife was not in good health and a few years after the marriage she died. To the disgust of his tenants, the Squire contacted Madeline who was living with her parents in London and asked her to come home again. This she did and lived with him at Crebilly for a good number of years, eventually bearing him a son. He suggested that she travel to London to show the child to her parents and whilst she was away, he married again, this time to a Miss Dufferin, who was the daughter of one of his footmen. She also bore him a son and Henry

Queen St. Terrace

instructed Madeline not to return. She did, however, come back to Ballymena when her parents died and it is said that she finished up begging on the streets there. When Henry himself died in 1875 aged only 46, his two sons began court action over what remained of his estate. After over a decade of legal wrangling, some of the lands of Crebilly went to Miss Dufferin's son, as the legitimate heir, but had to be sold off in order to meet legal debts. Miss Dufferin herself took what she could but married again to a very well-to-do man. Quite a contrast to the fate of poor Madeline.

There are also many stories told about the Squire O'Hara's foolishness. It is said that he used to fancy himself as something of a gambler and would arrange for grand card-playing evenings at Crebilly Castle. At these evenings, his fellow gamblers always made sure that he sat with his back to a mirror or reflective surface and in that way they could see what was in his hand. The Squire is said not to have realised what was going on and in this way, he gambled away most of the extensive family fortune and much of the Crebilly Estate. When he died, he was virtually penniless. In his time, he had been a good and much loved landlord who had built the village of Harryville (named after himself) mainly for his Catholic tenants.

He is buried in the churchyard at Ballyclug on the Larne Road and a monument, erected by his tenants who had tolerated and been amused by his eccentricities over the years, bears a formally broken tombstone – the symbol of 'decayed gentry' and one of the few places in Ireland where such a symbol can be found. The castle at Crebilly has long been pulled down but its gates remain and on certain nights in the week between Christmas and New Year, the ghost of the Squire O'Hara is said to ride on a white horse along the road between the back and front gates. Those who see him will be dead within the year, so this spectre is one to be avoided!

The church at Ballyclug itself has an interesting history. The name means 'the town of the bell' and an old legend states that when he was given his crozier by the angel Victor at the Skerry Church, Saint Patrick was also given a bell, which would ring when he was to found the second Christian church in Ireland (the church at Skerry being the first). As he approached the site at Ballyclug, the bell started to ring in his satchel, ringing louder and louder until the saint stopped. Some men were cutting stones nearby and St. Patrick used one of these as the cornerstone of his new church. Today, the church at Ballyclug is Church of Ireland, but is supposed to stand on the original site where the saint established his.

The villages of Harryville and Ballymena steadily grew towards each other and eventually merged. In 1937, the new town of Ballymena applied for Borough status and this was granted.

Travelling south from Ballymena, the landscape changes towards the valley of the Sixmilewater becoming a gentler, largely cultivated region of rolling hills and tilled fields, and the wild slopes of the Antrim Plateau with its Glens and rugged coastline are left far behind. Some say that this is 'where civilisation begins' but to suggest this is to ignore the wonderful, magical character of the mountain and coastal lands further north. In truth it is all part and parcel of the same wonderful area which looks to Ballymena as its capital.

Today, as Ballymena continues to expand with much building work going on around the edges of the town and in the surrounding villages, the future of the heart of North Antrim seems secure…

Conclusion

—: the old and the new :—

I set out to write this book in order to convey some of the awe, mystery and magic that I felt, as a child, about the land that lay around Ballymena and into the Glens of Antrim and about what made this area so special. However, as I worked through the text, I realised that the subject was so vast and so complex that in this book it would be possible to give only the merest glimpse of it. Indeed, it would take almost a whole library of books, coupled with an entire gallery of paintings to reflect the character, lore, people and the ever-changing moods of the region. Nevertheless, I hope that this volume has at least given a snapshot of a unique and wonderful land.

Nobody can ever really truly and completely know a place such as this. No matter how familiar we think we are with it, there is still some aspect of it – some perspective or some site hidden away from view – that can surprise, astonish and delight us. I am still finding out its secrets even yet. Only a few days ago, I stood in the middle of a busy builder's yard, not far from Ballymena, surrounded by machinery, bags of cement, and broken wooden pallets, looking at what was once the majestic gable wall of the medieval Kells Abbey with its thick stone walls and narrow chancel window. Just a little way further along was a small graveyard, containing a massive vault together with several gravestones belonging to now-vanished O'Hara lines. This lay beside and was obscured by, a parking area for lorries and mechanical diggers. My companions were two relatively local men – one from Ballycastle and the other from the Glens themselves – and for both of them it was their first visit to the place. Around us men came and went, delivering, collecting and moving building materials and yet the sense of history and tradition simply oozed from the stones of what had once been a very important monastic site. Similarly, I sat one evening with an old man, in his well-appointed kitchen away up in the Glens well above Carnlough as he told me tales of fairies and ghosts, which he believed, might still be found no more than a mile from his own modern bungalow. In the background, a widescreen television carried the news from distant parts of the world and a microwave defrosted something for his tea and yet, as I drove home through the oncoming twilight, the world of which he had spoken somehow seemed more real than the modern environment with all its technology and gadgetry. As evening drew on, I stopped by the roadside, on my way to Broughshane to look at a distant and dark clump of trees, tucked away in the corner of a field. A local woman had told me had once been the site of a church which had held a sacred relic, now lost, but before that had been the site of an even earlier pagan enclosure or fort. Modern people carriers passed by me on the road as I stood there, their radios blasting. And yet the sense of something far older and far more permanent than our own transient society, was particularly evident. It was something that is unquantifiable and which is also ultimately unknowable and in a sense this is the essence of the mystery and character of the area – a character which has emerged out of its history, legend and traditions.

That sense of timeless tradition has, of course, spread out into the wider Province and indeed in to the wider world. The Giant's Causeway and Slemish Mountain are two of Ireland's best-known geographical features and both of them are steeped in ancient legend and in ecclesiastical associations, which have attracted tourists and pilgrims from all over the world for many years. The natural beauty and wonderful isolation of the Glens have also been captured and extolled in both poetry and song, read and heard all across Ireland and further afield, again drawing travellers from many other places. Even as early as the late 1600s, visitors were coming to gaze in wonder and admiration at the Causeway or to journey into the then near impenetrable Glens. This region is still one of Northern Ireland's major tourist jewels.

The area covered in this book has sometimes been described as a 'world apart' and this is indeed a particularly apt description. It has been my intention to convey some of that 'separateness' and uniqueness through the history and lore, which hopefully complement Greg's excellent and evocative pictures.

I can only hope that, as a result of our efforts, you will visit this mystical and wonderful place and experience first-hand the magic and the sense of adventure which siezed a young boy's imagination and has never left me since.

Reflections of summer, Whitepark Bay

Dear Reader

This book is from our much complimented illustrated book series which includes:-

Belfast	Blanchardstown, Castleknock and the Park
By the Lough's North Shore	Dundrum, Stillorgan & Rathfarnham
East Belfast	Blackrock, Dún Laoghaire, Dalkey
South Belfast	Bray and North Wicklow
Antrim, Town & Country	Dublin's North Coast
Inishowen	Limerick's Glory
Donegal Highlands	Galway on the Bay
Donegal, South of the Gap	Connemara
Donegal Islands	The Book of Clare
Islands of Connaught	Kildare
Sligo	Carlow
Mayo	Armagh
Fermanagh	Ring of Gullion
Omagh	Carlingford Lough
Cookstown	The Mournes
Dundalk & North Louth	Heart of Down
Drogheda & the Boyne Valley	Strangford's Shore

Cottage Publications

Cottage Publications
is an imprint of
Laurel Cottage Ltd
15 Ballyhay Road
Donaghadee, Co. Down
N. Ireland, BT21 0NG

For the more athletically minded our illustrated walking book series includes:-

Bernard Davey's Mourne   Bernard Davey's Mourne Part 2   Tony McAuley's Glens

Also available in our 'Illustrated History & Companion' Range are:-

Ballymoney   Banbridge

And from our Music series:-

Colum Sands, Between the Earth and the Sky

We can also supply prints, individually signed by the artist, of the paintings featured in the above titles as well as many other areas of Ireland.

For details on these superb publications and to view samples of the paintings they contain, you can visit our web site at **www.cottage-publications.com** or alternatively you can contact us as follows:-

Telephone: +44 (028) 9188 8033   Fax: +44 (028) 9188 8063